STILL MORE IT HAPPENED IN HOCKEY

STILL MORE WEIRD & WONDERFUL STORIES
FROM CANADA'S GREATEST GAME

BRIAN McFARLANE

D1530500

Stoddart

Published in 1994 by
Stoddart Publishing Co. Limited
34 Lesmill Road
Toronto, Canada
M3B 2T6
(416) 445-3333

Canadian Cataloguing in Publication Data

McFarlane, Brian, 1931–
Still more it happened in hockey

ISBN 0-7737-5685-X

1. Hockey — Canada. I. Title.

GV848.4.C3M34 1994   796.962'0971   C94-931178-2

Cover Design: Leslie Styles
Typesetting: Tony Gordon Ltd.
Printed and bound in Canada

*Stoddart Publishing gratefully acknowledges the
support of the Canada Council, Ontario Ministry of
Culture, Tourism, and Recreation, Ontario Arts Council,
and Ontario Publishing Centre in the development of
writing and publishing in Canada.*

CONTENTS

PART 1 — Titans of the Rink

PART 2 — Off-ice Overseers and Pundits

PART 3 — Battlers and Warriors

PART 4 — Tales and Tidbits from the Past

PART 5 — Curious Capers

PART

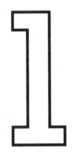

TITANS OF
THE RINK

Lafleur Was Fast Off the Ice

WHEN THE MONTREAL CANADIENS were winning four consecutive Stanley Cups from 1976 to 1979, their fastest skater and most prolific scorer was Guy (Flower) Lafleur. One night the superstar's fast pace off the ice almost cost him his life.

Postgame partying was something Lafleur enjoyed, and there were always friends and teammates willing to share his penchant for liquor, rock music, and endless cigarettes. When the partying was over, he would race home at dizzying speeds in his Cadillac Seville. But in the early-morning hours of March 25, 1981, Lafleur fell asleep behind the wheel and near disaster followed. His powerful

When the Montreal Canadiens swept to four straight Stanley Cups from 1976 to 1979, Guy Lafleur was their ace scorer, winning three consecutive scoring titles.
(Robert B. Shaver)

3

vehicle roared off the highway and plunged down an embankment, smashing into a metal post that shattered the windshield. Part of the post, twisted into something resembling a knight's lance, missed Lafleur's head by a fraction of an inch and sliced off part of his right ear. He was lucky to come out of the accident alive.

Lafleur had already established a reputation for high-speed driving. In 1978, according to *The Hockey News,* he reached speeds of 177 miles per hour while driving his Ferrari the 150-mile distance from Montreal to Quebec City.

After his brush with death in 1981, Lafleur promised to change his lifestyle. "I decided to slow down after that," he said. "I realized that my family was more important to me than downtown nightlife."

When Espo First Met Mr. Hockey

PHIL ESPOSITO HAS A VIVID MEMORY of the night he played against Gordie Howe for the first time.

"I'll never forget it," he told me recently. "It was my first game in the NHL. Well, my second one actually, because I sat on the bench throughout my first game, which was against Montreal at the Forum. I almost got to play in that game. With two minutes to play we [Chicago] were losin' 7–2. Coach Billy Reay looks down the bench and yells, 'Esposito, get out there!'

"Well, I was disappointed I hadn't taken a single shift, so I shouted, 'Okay, Coach, do you want me to win it or tie it?'

4

"He yelled back, 'Sit down, smartass.'

"Two nights later we're in Detroit, and who do I find myself standin' next to when I get on the ice but Gordie Howe. Geez, he was my boyhood hero. I'm lookin' at Gordie and I'm sayin' to myself, Damn, that's the great Gordie Howe. What am I doin' out here?

"Just before we're ready to face off, Bobby Hull yells at me, 'Watch that old son of a bitch!' With that Gordie blinks once or twice and gets a little grin on his face, and that's when the puck is dropped. I'm still lookin' at him, thinkin' this is unbelievable, when bam! he gives me an elbow in the mouth.

"I stagger back and say, 'Why, you old fart, you!' Then I spear him a good one and we both get penalties.

"In those days, in the penalty box, the players sat close together with a cop or an usher or somebody in between them. So I'm sittin' there holdin' a towel to my split lip and I'm real upset with big Howe. Without thinking, I lean across the guy between us and say to Gordie, 'To think you *used* to be my bleepin' idol.'

"Howe snarls back, 'What did you say, rookie?'

"Quickly I say, 'Nothin', Mr. Howe, not a word.'

"To this day, I'll never forget that look."

How the Leafs Lost Two Future Stars

IN 1932 THE TORONTO MAPLE LEAFS captured the Stanley Cup, and for the next few years owner Conn Smythe relied on the nucleus of that team. But soon younger, fresher players were needed.

In western Canada Leaf scout Beattie Ramsay phoned Smythe and told him he was sending three bright prospects to the 1938 Leaf training camp. He was certain Smythe would be impressed with at least two of the three men he was sending. Their names were Doug Bentley and Elmer Lach. The third player was Harvey Barnes.

At training camp the shy young westerners were all but ignored by the other Leafs. No one knew much about them, except that Beattie Ramsay had recommended them. The boys were awed by the big city and intimidated by the reputations of the men who dressed next to them for the training camp scrimmages. Many of the Leafs — stars like Conacher, Primeau, Jackson, and Horner — had been their boyhood idols. In the workouts the westerners felt awkward and self-conscious. They found it difficult to fit in with the famous NHL players.

Into the dressing room one day strode Leaf owner Conn Smythe. After kibitzing with his regulars, he noticed the trio of rookies huddled in a corner.

"I thought Beattie Ramsay was sending me some men," he snorted. "Looks like he sent me three little peanuts instead."

Some of the Leafs laughed, others felt badly about Smythe's putdown.

"Don't worry about it, kids," one of them said. "Mr. Smythe is always popping off. None of us will get swollen heads so long as he's around."

But Smythe's words had left the boys from the West dazed and humiliated.

The next morning they didn't show up for practice. When coach Dick Irvin called their hotel, he was told they had left the city.

"They said they were going back home, Mr. Irvin. They took last night's train for Regina."

It was true. Lach, Bentley, and Barnes all vowed they would play hockey as far away from Toronto as possible. And they did — for a year or two. Then Bentley got a break with the Chicago Blackhawks and soon became a star, scoring 33 goals and 73 points in the 1942–43 season. He told the Hawks he had a brother Max who was "even better than me" and brought him to training camp. Soon the Bentleys and Bill Mosienko formed the Pony Line, one of the highest scoring lines in hockey.

Elmer Lach, meanwhile, had distanced himself from the Leafs by playing with the Moose Jaw Millers. It wasn't long before his stylish play caught the eye of Paul Haynes, a Montreal scout. In 1940 Lach headed east for another training camp, and this time he had no trouble catching on with the famous Montreal Canadiens. Coach Dick Irvin, who had left Toronto to become the mentor of the Habs, was delighted to see Lach again, one of Smythe's "little peanuts." And thankful for Conn Smythe's acid tongue and the words that had driven young Lach away from Toronto.

In time Lach, too, helped form a famous line, the renowned Punch Line of Lach, Toe Blake, and Maurice Richard. With Lach in the the lineup for the next 13 years, the Habs rolled to four consecutive first-place finishes and captured three Stanley Cups.

It would be nice to report that Harvey Barnes, the third "little peanut," found big league stardom, too. Alas, it was not to be. But two out of three isn't bad.

7

Bossy Had a Backer

THE DAY BEFORE THE 1977 entry draft meetings got under way, New York Islander scout Henry Saraceno walked into general manager Bill Torrey's office, took a picture off the wall, and replaced it with a large color portrait of Mike Bossy. The message was clear — Saraceno was pleading with Torrey to select Bossy in the upcoming draft. For weeks Saraceno had been trying to convince Torrey to grab the teenage sniper from the Laval Nationals of the Quebec Major Junior League. He told his boss repeatedly that if he signed Bossy he would never regret it.

But Torrey had heard some disturbing things about the shooter from Laval. There was no doubt he could score goals, but he was a skinny kid and prone to injuries. Even more, his defensive play was suspect and he disliked fighting with a passion. Those raps had to be considered.

Saraceno reminded Torrey that he had been Bossy's coach one year in Peewee hockey and the kid had once scored 15 goals in a single period. He talked of Bossy's 309 goals in his Junior career — only five fewer than Guy Lafleur.

"Take him, Bill. He'll burn up the league."

"I don't know, Henry. It's a tough decision. Besides, he may not be around when I get to draft. Remember, we're number 15 on the list."

On draft day 14 Juniors were selected — among them six right wingers — and Bossy was still available. Obviously the other clubs had scouted him well and were concerned about his deficiencies.

Torrey took a deep breath, made up his mind, and

announced, "The New York Islanders select Mike Bossy, right winger with Laval."

No one in hockey — not even Bossy himself — was more elated than Saraceno when Torrey made his choice.

"I'm sure it was the happiest day of Henry Saraceno's life," Torrey would say at his scout's funeral two years later. "Others doubted Mike, but Henry never did. He had absolute faith that Mike would become one of hockey's greatest scorers."

Bossy, too, had confidence in his ability to put the puck in the net. When Torrey signed him to a contract, the GM asked the 20-year-old rookie how many goals he planned to score.

"I should get 50" was the reply.

"Fifty!" Torrey exclaimed. "No rookie has ever scored 50."

"Well, I think I will."

And he did. He pumped home 20 goals in his first 22 games and established a rookie record for goal scoring with 53. The previous record holder was Buffalo's Richard Martin with 44.

Fifty-goal seasons became Bossy's trademark. In nine seasons as an Islander he never scored fewer than 50 — a feat no other player, not even Wayne Gretzky, has achieved. He would easily have completed a 10th 50-goal season had not a back injury hampered his play and forced him into early retirement.

His rookie record of 53 goals lasted until 1992–93 when Teemu Selanne of the Winnipeg Jets established a new mark of 76. But 50 goals or more for nine consecutive years? That record should stand for a long time.

If Henry Saraceno were around to comment, he would no doubt say, "I'm so proud of Michael and his accomplishments. All the records he set, the All-Star teams, the four Stanley Cups, the Hall of Fame. But then I knew he could do it all the time. I'm glad Bill Torrey listened to me."

A Night for Johnny — Halfway Through His Career

IN 1968 THE BOSTON BRUINS held a night for veteran left winger Johnny Bucyk, one of their most popular players. Bucyk had served the Bruins well for a dozen seasons, but his goal production had slipped to 18 the previous year and retirement seemed imminent. Bucyk accepted the new car, the outboard motor, and the other gifts, as well as the plaudits for serving the Bruins so well for so long.

There was just one hitch. At age 32 Bucyk had no intention of retiring. To prove he hadn't lost his scoring touch, he recorded a 30-goal season. Then, like a kid starting all over again, he scored 24 goals, 31 goals and, incredibly, 51 goals. At age 35 he had become the only player of that vintage to score 50 goals or more in a season.

Bucyk still gave no thought to retirement. Five years later, at age 40, he potted 36 goals. Only when he turned 43 did he decide it was time to step aside . . . after a "disappointing" 20-goal season.

More than 10 years had passed since he had been honored on Johnny Bucyk Night at the Boston Garden. The car and the outboard had long since worn out. But not John. He had stayed around for two Stanley Cup victories plus several individual honors, including a pair of Lady Byng trophies. He had scored another 319 goals since his "retirement" party and had become the fourth-leading scorer of all time with 556 markers.

No wonder he was swiftly inducted into the Hockey Hall of Fame in 1981.

That'll Be 30 Bucks, Mr. Day

WHEN HAP DAY, a star player for the Toronto Maple Leafs in the late 1920s, signed his contract with Conn Smythe one year, he noticed an unusual clause in the pact. It stated: "The hockey club shall furnish the player with a complete hockey uniform with the player placing a $30 deposit with the club, said deposit to be returned to the player at the end of the season upon the return of the uniform."

Fan Claims Vezina Wore No Gloves

BACK IN 1968 J. TUDOR, an elderly hockey fan from Perth, Ontario, wrote me a letter in which he described early-day hockey at Dey's Arena in Ottawa. Here is an interesting excerpt:

I could tell you some amusing stories about those oldtimers. For example, I saw Cyclone Taylor score that famous goal while he was skating backwards.

My brother and I used to go to all the games played at Dey's Arena. Believe me, it was worse than a barn. The wind would whistle through the cracks in the boards and I'm sure it must have been warmer standing out in the middle of the Rideau Canal. My brother and I would stand in behind the wire netting back of the goal when the Montreal team was playing the Ottawas. We'd bring pea-shooters to the game and we fired peas at Georges Vezina's head whenever an Ottawa player came in to take a shot on goal.

Vezina couldn't speak English but he sure knew how to curse in French. After a time he got wise and pulled a small cap over his head. He would pull the cap around with the peak at the back to deflect the peas we'd shoot, aiming for the back of his neck. That cap robbed us of a lovely target.

Vezina wore no gloves. He had a great pair of hands. The players today are sissies compared to the oldtimers. They are only on the ice a minute or two. In the old days, a man would play the full sixty minutes without relief. And sometimes overtime.

I remember a great player named Ching Johnston, a defenseman. He used to stop plays by stretching out full length on the ice. The only way to get around him was to flip the puck in, leap over him and go after it. He was tough and rugged. I saw him play once with his face completely covered by bandages. I mean covered. Only his eyes and mouth could be seen. Those were the good old days when they had better players and games than they have today.

In those days the rush end seats cost only fifteen cents. The goal judge stood on a board on the ice right behind the goal. Many times a player, usually the rover, would dash in and send him flying, especially if the puck was being shot at the Ottawa goal. This prevented the goal judge from seeing whether the puck went in or not.

I should point out that the game in which Cyclone Taylor was alleged to have scored a goal while skating backward took place in Renfrew, not Dey's Arena in Ottawa. I still find it difficult to believe that Georges Vezina ever played without gloves but will accept the testimony of an eyewitness.

Vezina Was a Remarkable Man

GEORGES VEZINA, WHOSE MEMORY is perpetuated in the Vezina Trophy, enjoyed a brilliant 15-year career in professional hockey. The Montreal Canadiens discovered him one night in 1910 when they played an exhibition game in Chicoutimi, Vezina's hometown. Vezina, already nicknamed the Chicoutimi Cucumber for his coolness under fire, stopped the mighty Habs without a goal in that game. By the time the next season rolled around, he had signed a professional contract with Montreal.

For the next decade and a half Vezina served as the Canadiens' regular netminder. Incredibly, though, he didn't learn how to skate until he was in his late teens. Until then he preferred to tend goal wearing his everyday shoes or boots. It was only two years prior to his pro debut with Montreal that he appeared on the ice wearing skates.

13

Vezina married young, at age 20, and then raised a whopping big family of 22 children. One of his offspring was born on the night the Montreal Canadiens won the Stanley Cup in 1916. To mark the occasion, the infant was named Stanley. Fortunately it was a baby boy.

On November 28, 1925, in Montreal's home opener, Vezina took his place in goal for a game against Pittsburgh. He had been feeling poorly for some time, but on this night he was gravely ill. Before the game his temperature reached 105 degrees. But he insisted on playing and managed to get through one period before collapsing on the ice. He was carried off, never to return. Doctors told him he was suffering from an advanced case of tuberculosis. The great goaltender died four months later in Chicoutimi, the town he loved and had made famous.

Stranger to the Sin Bin

VAL FONTEYNE WAS A SKINNY LITTLE GUY, a dandy penalty killer for the Detroit Red Wings, the New York Rangers, and the Pittsburgh Penguins in the sixties and early seventies. Most penalty killers, because their sole objective is to stop the opposing team's top scorers, are often tenants of the penalty box themselves. They know all the obstruction tricks, like holding, hooking, and interference — infractions that seldom go unnoticed.

But Val Fonteyne avoided penalty boxes as if they were snake pits. He played five consecutive years without ever being in one. In his 13-year career, which encompassed 820 regular season games, he served a mere 28 minutes in penalty time. He took a career high of eight minutes in 1964–65, which for him was akin to being a hardened criminal.

Mario Disrupts the Draft Routine

AT THE NHL entry draft meetings in 1984, Pittsburgh Penguin general manager Eddie Johnston placed teenager Mario Lemieux head and shoulders above all other eligible players. With first choice in the annual lottery, Johnston had been negotiating with Lemieux's agents for weeks. By June 9, draft day at the Montreal Forum, they had been unable to agree on what Lemieux was worth.

Johnston was in an awkward position. He was counting on Lemieux to save the Penguin franchise. He had agreed to allow a live feed of the draft proceedings to be televised back to Pittsburgh where thousands of Penguin fans had bought tickets for the event, just for the privilege of seeing Lemieux don the Penguins colors for the very first time.

Over the years a popular ritual has been observed by players selected in the entry draft. When the player's name is called, he rises from his seat, hugs and kisses his family members, walks across the arena floor to greet his new employers, and slips on a team jersey while dozens of cameramen record the big moment for posterity.

That was the moment, and the reaction, the fans in Pittsburgh counted on and waited for — to see Lemieux face the cameras and say how happy he was to be a Penguin, how he hoped to lead them to the playoffs and the Stanley Cup. Johnston, always a realist, could only cross his fingers and pray for such a moment.

When Johnston announced in French and English, "The Pittsburgh Penguins select Mario Lemieux from the Laval Voisins," the TV cameras zoomed in on Lemieux. He stood, a solemn look on his face, waved at the crowd, and sat down. Pittsburgh fans were stunned and Johnston looked glum. It was a clear message from Lemieux to the general manager. "I will not come to your table and put on your Pittsburgh jersey because you don't appear to want me very badly. If you did, you would be willing to pay me what I know I am worth."

Meanwhile the fans watching at the Civic Arena in Pittsburgh began booing the screen and howling their frustration. Some were angry at Lemieux, calling him a prima donna, while others cursed the Penguins for not opening the purse strings and giving the money his agent demanded.

Back at the Forum a member of the Penguins' staff rushed to where Lemieux was sitting and urged him to reconsider. "Mario, come down to our table," he pleaded. Mario told the chap to get lost.

Reporters took sides. Some criticized Mario's stance, others applauded him for sticking up for his beliefs. In less than a week everyone involved was able to breathe a sigh of relief. Mario's agents negotiated a two-year contract worth a reported $700,000. He received a signing bonus of $150,000, and there were additional bonus amounts he would be able to achieve based on attendance increases in Pittbsurgh.

Lemieux was on his way. At last he was able to don the Pittsburgh jersey and wear it proudly.

16

Milt Schmidt Signs with Boston

WHEN MILT SCHMIDT FIRST ATTRACTED the attention of the Boston Bruins, he was a naive 17-year-old from Kitchener, Ontario. Invited to the Boston training camp, he wrote Bruin manager Art Ross and told him he would get a summer job immediately so that he could pay his way to the team's training quarters in Hershey. Ross chuckled about that letter in later years. "Miltie was so green," he said, "he didn't know the team picked up all travel expenses."

"Oh, I was green, all right," Schmidt told me recently. "Especially when Ross called me in to sign my first contract with the Bruins. He offered me something like $3,000, and I told him I'd like $3,500. Well, he raised his eyebrows and said that was more than he'd been authorized to give me. He said he'd have to go down the hall and discuss my request with the team owner, Mr. Adams. So I waited patiently while he went to see Mr. Adams. In a few minutes he was back, and he had a grim look on his face. 'Sorry, Milt,' he said, 'I fought for you, but Mr. Adams wouldn't budge on the $3,000 offer. He told me you could take it or leave it.'

"So I reached for a pen and signed the contract. On my way out of the building I passed Mr. Adams's office. I said to myself, I think I'll go in there and ask Mr. Adams why he wouldn't give me the extra 500 bucks I requested. So I entered the office and encountered Mr. Adams's secretary.

"'Yes? Can I help you?' she asked.

"'Hi. I'm Milt Schmidt. I just signed with the Bruins and I'd like to see Mr. Adams, please.'

Boston's celebrated Kraut Line: Bobby Bauer (left), Milt Schmidt, and Woody Dumart. (National Archives of Canada)

"She smiled and said, 'I'm sorry, but Mr. Adams isn't in today. He won't be in all week.'"

Milt turned to me. "Brian," he said, "they lied to me from day one, and they've been lying to me ever since."

He Led Three Teams in Scoring . . . in Three Consecutive Seasons

NO PLAYER IN THE NHL had ever led three different teams in scoring in consecutive seasons . . . until Vincent Damphousse accomplished the unusual feat in 1992–93. Damphousse was the top scorer in Toronto's lineup in 1990–91 with 73 points. Then he was traded to

Edmonton, where he collected a team-high 89 points the following season. Another trade sent him to the Montreal Canadiens, and once again he topped all his teammates with 97 points. The only other player to lead three different teams in scoring, but not in consecutive years, is retired pro Lanny McDonald, who was his team's scoring leader in Toronto, Colorado, and Calgary.

Benedict's Brilliance Still Doesn't Bring Him the Cup

IN THE 1928 STANLEY CUP PLAYOFFS, goalie Clint Benedict of the Montreal Maroons played the best hockey of his career. Game after game he was sensational. In the first round, a two-game series against Ottawa, he shut out the Senators 1–0 in game one and was almost as stingy in game two, winning 2–1. Then he faced the first-place Montreal Canadiens in another two-game series. His Maroons tied the first game 2–2 and won the second 1–0. In the final series against the Rangers, Benedict racked up his third playoff shutout in the opener, winning 1–0. Game two, a 2–1 Ranger triumph, will long be remembered as the game in which 44-year-old Lester Patrick, the Ranger coach, took over in goal when his regular goaltender was injured. The Rangers beat Benedict and the Maroons in overtime that night by 2–1. Benedict bounced back with his fourth playoff shutout (2–0) in game three, but the Rangers, with Miller in goal, returned the compliment and shut down the Maroons 1–0 in game four. New York captured game five 2–1 and skated off with the Stanley Cup.

19

Nobody blamed Clint Benedict for the Maroons' defeat. He had compiled four shutouts in nine games and allowed a mere eight goals. His near-perfect netminding was reflected in his goals-against average — a minuscule 0.89.

It was a brilliant record. Unfortunately, not brilliant enough to get his name on the Stanley Cup.

Larry Robinson Starred in Football, Too

AFTER MORE THAN 20 SEASONS in professional hockey, Larry Robinson, now an assistant coach with New Jersey, has enough fond memories of the game to last him a lifetime. But if you ask him to recall one of the biggest thrills in his sporting life, the conversation might turn to football and games played during his youth at tiny Osgoode Township High School, located a few miles from Ottawa.

He told me once: "Hockey was my first love when I was growing up in Marvellville, Ontario. I attended a one-room schoolhouse, and when winter came, all the kids would pitch in and make a rink. In the play area beside the school we'd wet down the snow with a hose and then pack it down by tramping on it with our boots. That made the base. Then we'd flood our little rink all night long, building up layers of ice. Two or three of us would sleep in the school while the rest would be out working on the rink. By morning we'd have great ice.

"While hockey was number one with me, I changed sports with the seasons. I attended Osgoode Township High School and remember when I registered there how upset I was to learn the school had no gymnasium. In my third year there a gym was added and we helped christen it by winning the Ontario basketball championship. There were only about 300 students in the school, but we had a lot of good athletes.

"You won't believe the football team we had. In my final year at Osgoode our football team scored 200 points and didn't give up a single point. It was incredible. I've never heard of another Canadian high school team with such a record. I played corner linebacker and tight end offensively. Most of our players went both ways. Our team even took part in a football tournament where all the teams involved played two 15-minute periods. We won the first period 12–0 and the second 14–0. In the finals we won again, 16–0. Even with all my good memories of hockey, I can never forget that season in football. Undefeated, untied, unscored on. You can't do any better than that. I'm sure there are fans in the Ottawa Valley who still talk about that team."

Freak Injury Almost Crippled Mark Howe

IT HAPPENED, AS MOST THINGS DO IN HOCKEY, in an instant. On December 27, 1980, the Hartford Whalers were hosting the New York Islanders. There was a close play at the net, and the Isles' John Tonelli crashed into Whaler defenseman Mark Howe. The net slipped off its moorings and was tilted back by the force of the collision. Howe lost his balance, flew backward into the net, and impaled himself on the sharp metal prong that acts as a puck deflector. The prong was sticking up, and about five and a half inches of it sliced through Howe's hockey pants and penetrated his buttocks, stopping just short of the rectal wall and the spinal column.

Bleeding heavily and in great pain, Howe required immediate medical attention. But there was no ambulance at the Hartford Civic Center that night, and precious time was lost until one arrived and whisked Howe to a nearby hospital. A call was made to the Howe family physician, Dr. DeMaio, but an hour passed before he arrived at the hospital. Told that Mark had suffered a laceration, the doctor was aghast when he saw the extent of the wound. It might easily be described as life-threatening.

If the metal prong had penetrated the rectal wall, there was a risk of peritonitis. The wound was dangerously close to the intestines, which could have led to infection. Another half inch and it would have hit the spinal column, which meant that Howe might never have walked again. Had the prong cut through the sphincter muscle Howe might have lost control of his bowel movements.

The physician-surgeon cleaned and closed the wound and prescribed large doses of antibiotics. Howe made an astonishing recovery and returned to action with the Whalers in early February.

The NHL launched an immediate investigation, and within days NHL clubs were making changes in their goal nets, trimming and beveling the dangerous prong or centerpiece.

Cory Gurnsey Finds a Big League Pal

ON A WINTER DAY IN 1980 Cory Gurnsey, a nine-year-old Calgary boy, was walking home from school when he was brutally assaulted and stabbed several times. Destroyed in the attack was Cory's beloved hockey jersey, a Montreal Canadiens sweater with Guy Lafleur's number 10 sewn on the back.

It wasn't long before the Montreal Canadiens heard about Cory's plight, and within a day or two a brand-new Guy Lafleur sweater was delivered to his hospital room. Guy himself phoned the hospital to talk with Cory and to wish him a speedy recovery. He even promised to score a goal for Cory in an upcoming game between Montreal and Toronto. Of course, he kept his promise. Then he had the puck mounted on a plaque, autographed it, and mailed it to Cory.

But there was an even bigger surprise in store for Cory. When the young man recovered sufficiently to travel, he was flown to Montreal to see his hockey hero in action — as a guest of the Canadiens and Guy Lafleur. Against Vancouver that night Lafleur scored another goal, once again keeping a promise to his young friend. In the weeks ahead, whenever the Canadiens visited Calgary, Cory could rely on at least a phone call and sometimes a luncheon invitation from the man who had taken such an interest in his well-being.

Of the 518 goals Lafleur scored in his career, two will never be forgotten by Cory Gurnsey of Calgary. Those were the two dedicated to him — by one of the greatest goal scorers of all time.

The Stingy Scot

CHARLIE GARDINER SHOULD BE HIGH on the list of hockey's best all-time goaltenders. He was born in Scotland and learned to play hockey in Winnipeg. In the NHL he toiled for the woeful Chicago Blackhawks in the late twenties and early thirties. It wasn't Charlie's fault his team won only seven games each season during his first two years on the job. In seven seasons he won the Vezina Trophy twice and was named to the first All-Star team three times.

Year after year Gardiner was the best of a sorry lot, and when the 1933–34 season rolled around, Charlie had almost given up his dream of playing in the Stanley Cup spotlight. The Chicago scorers were pitiful that season, totaling only 88 goals, the lowest production in the NHL.

But somehow the Blackhawks found themselves in the playoffs, and that was when Gardiner decided he better come up with some of his best efforts. Playoff action was heady stuff for Chicago. It might be his one and only chance for hockey glory. In the days ahead his play was truly spectacular as he guided his team past the Canadiens and then the Maroons.

Only the Detroit Red Wings stood between the Hawks and Lord Stanley's old mug. Most hockey men didn't give the upstarts from Chicago a chance against the Red Wings. After all, they hadn't won a game in Detroit in four years, and the first two games of the final series were scheduled for the Olympia.

Even Roger Jenkins, one of Gardiner's teammates, downgraded his own team's chances. He bet Gardiner no goalie could stop the Wings. "If you do,

24

I'll wheel you around the Loop in Chicago in a wheelbarrow," he promised.

Another teammate, Alex Levinsky, had lost faith earlier than that. He put his wife on a train for Toronto when the playoffs began and packed all his clothes in his car. "See you in a few days, hon," he told her. For the next month he kept dragging a change of clothes out of the trunk of his car.

Gardiner turned in an outstanding performance in the opener of the best-of-five final series as the Hawks won 2–1. He added another solid effort two nights later, winning 4–1. The Red Wings fought back on Chicago ice and beat him 5–2, while the fourth game in this best-of-five final required more than 30 minutes of overtime before Chicago's Mush March connected for the Stanley Cup-winning goal.

The low-scoring Hawks had captured their first Cup, and Charlie Gardiner, the stingy Scot, had realized his dream. Two days later he climbed aboard a wheelbarrow and enjoyed a bumpy ride around the Loop, with Roger Jenkins providing the horsepower.

Two months later the cheering stopped. Back home in Winnipeg the popular 30-year-old netminder suffered a brain hemorrhage and died shortly after being admitted to hospital.

Emotions Ran High When McDonald Was Traded

ON A DECEMBER DAY IN 1979 hockey fans in Toronto were stunned to hear that Lanny McDonald, an all-time favorite Maple Leaf, had been traded to Colorado for Wilf Paiement and Pat Hickey. The news was just as devastating inside the Leaf dressing room, where players felt the trade was a vindictive move by general manager Punch Imlach, one that would sting team captain Darryl Sittler in particular. Sittler was Lanny's linemate and best friend and both were at odds with Imlach.

After a meeting with Punch, McDonald entered the Leaf dressing room holding a flight schedule to Colorado. Tears filled his eyes and he was unable to speak. Sittler took the schedule from him, glanced at it, and he, too, began to cry. Other Leafs, having guessed the bad news, started to choke up, and more tears fell. Then anger took over and players began cursing Imlach and throwing equipment around the dressing room. Socks, jockstraps, and towels flew through the air. Mirrors and walls were sprayed with shaving cream, and soon the room was a shambles.

Tiger Williams, who would soon be traded himself, said later: "It was one of the most emotional scenes I'd ever seen. Plain and simple, we went on a rampage. And then Rocky Saganiuk, a cocky rookie, spoke up. Said he would replace McDonald on right wing. That really pissed us off."

A few days later in Winnipeg the Leaf players, led by Williams, grabbed Saganiuk after a practice. They stripped and shaved him, then strapped him to a table and pushed it out to center ice, leaving him there and going out to lunch.

The Last Goalie to Do It

THE LAST GOALTENDER TO PLAY in every one of his team's games in a single season was Boston's Ed Johnston in 1963–64. The NHL schedule encompassed 70 games in that era.

We all know that Jacques Plante popularized the goalie face mask in 1959. The last goaltender to play in the NHL without wearing a mask was Andy Brown, who toiled for Pittsburgh and Detroit from 1971 to 1974.

The last goaltender to play an entire All-Star game was Chicago's Glenn Hall, who led his All-Star mates to a victory over the Montreal Canadiens, the defending Cup champions, in 1965.

The last non-goalie to stand in goal during an NHL game, substituting for an injured goaltender, was Boston's Gerry Toppazinni. He took over for Don Simmons in the dying seconds of a game on October 6, 1960. Boston lost the match 4–1.

The Day Grove Sutton Outshone Wayne Gretzky

WAYNE GRETZKY WILL REMEMBER the game as one of the most important of his career. He will recall the bitter disappointment in the dressing room and how he hung his head and cried after his team lost by five goals. Personally he had done well, scoring a goal and collecting three assists. But Grove Sutton, a star player on the opposing team, had done even better, scoring five goals in leading his team to a 9–4 victory.

Grove Sutton? Outscoring Gretzky? I must be kidding, you say. Where and when did this happen?

It was 1974, and there was more than the normal excitement and hype to the 15th Annual Quebec Peewee Hockey Tournament. Wayne Gretzky, the tiny tornado from Brantford, was the biggest story at the event. Everyone had heard reports about his amazing scoring exploits and how he had bagged 378 goals in one season alone when he was 10 years old and only four foot four. Children much bigger and older than he sought his autograph, and over 10,000 fans turned out to see him play in his first tournament game.

Brantford humiliated a terrified group of youngsters from Richardson, Texas, 25–0 in game one. The Americans were hockey novices. They had never seen slap shots before, never played at this level, and seldom played before more than a handful of people. Their goalie was so frightened he couldn't perform, and a teammate who had never worn goal pads before had to take his place in the net.

During the game, Gretzky scored seven goals and added four assists for 11 points, breaking Guy Lafleur's single-game tournament record by one. He followed up with two goals and three assists in Brantford's 9–1 victory over Beaconsfield, Quebec. Game three was against Verdun, Quebec, led by a flashy little centerman named Denis Savard. Fan interest was so high that Gretzky had to battle his way through the crowds to the dressing room. With a policeman's help he finally reached his destination and had to hurry into his uniform. Brantford won again 7–3 with Wayne notching three goals.

His next test — in the tournament semifinals — was against a team from Oshawa, Ontario, a solid club that had often spelled trouble for the Brantford boys in the past. Wayne played both defense and forward and collected a goal and three assists, but Oshawa had a swift-skating Peewee named Grove Sutton, a heads-up player who outshone

Wayne with five goals in the 9–4 Oshawa victory. Sutton wasn't just a one-game wonder, either, for he collected 17 goals in the tournament, four more than Gretzky. And in the championship game Sutton led his team to the Peewee title with a victory over Peterborough.

At the time few could have foreseen that Wayne Gretzky, or "le Grand Gretzky" as he was called, would grow up to become hockey's greatest scorer. Just as no one could have predicted that Grove Sutton would soon fade from the hockey scene, only to be remembered by the fans who had witnessed his greatest week in hockey, the week he outscored Wayne Gretzky, the most talked-about young player in the game.

Why Coffey Missed Orr's Record

IT WAS THE FINAL GAME OF THE 1985–86 NHL season and Paul Coffey of the Edmonton Oilers was awfully close to tying or breaking Bobby Orr's remarkable record for a defenseman — 139 points in a season. Trailing by a point in the season finale against Vancouver, it figured that Coffey would be a shoo-in to establish a new mark. But he soon discovered there were factors involved that might prevent him from reaching his goal. Bob McCammon, then an Oiler assistant coach, revealed the reason for Coffey's failure to displace Orr months after the incident, when he joined the Canucks as head coach.

"In that final game with Vancouver, Glen Sather wanted to keep the score down, win the game, and avoid meeting Calgary in the first round of the playoffs. Paul began rushing with the puck, looking for points, and taking chances. Finally Sather benched him."

The benching was the start of a rift between Coffey and his coach. Coffey finished the game pointless and wound up with 138 points to Orr's 139.

Fortunately Coffey was able to take some satisfaction in smashing another of Orr's long-standing records — 47 goals in a season for a defenseman. Coffey finished with 48.

Jacques Plante's Amazing Comeback

AFTER THE 1964–65 NHL SEASON, Jacques Plante, one of the NHL's greatest goaltenders, decided to retire from hockey. He was 37 years old and he had lost his starting position with the New York Rangers — first to Marcel Paille and then to Gilles Villemure. A proud man, Plante had even been sent to the minors, and that enraged him.

There were other problems facing Plante. A bad knee required surgery and his wife was quite ill. Her weight had dropped from 128 to 98 pounds, and the doctors feared she was on the verge of a nervous breakdown. Plante's two boys, aged 10 and 14, had grown up virtually without a father because of his frequent long absences from home.

So Plante quit hockey and began working for the Molson brewery in Montreal. He also did part-time work for the CBC and for a newspaper. Each week he chipped in $2.50 to play pickup hockey with a group of old-timers.

Jacques Plante stands tough minus stick, ready for all comers.

(National Archives of Canada)

Then, on December 16, 1965, he was invited by coach Scotty Bowman to tend goal in an exhibition game at the Montreal Forum, playing for a Junior team against the vaunted Soviet national squad. Plante was superb in the contest. Veteran columnist Andy O'Brien called his performance "the greatest single display of skilled goaling I have ever seen."

Three seasons passed and Bowman, now coach and general manager of the St. Louis Blues, was looking for an experienced goaltender. He had never forgotten the game in which Plante had stunned the Soviets. At the 1968 NHL draft meetings in Montreal, Bowman shocked the hockey world by selecting Plante, the 40-year-old has-been. Bowman had no concerns about Plante's age. In the previous season, 37-year-old Glenn Hall had taken the Blues to the Stanley Cup finals, and Hall had capped his season by winning the Conn Smythe Trophy as playoff MVP.

After being drafted, Plante decided to have arthroscopic surgery on his wonky knee. Then he started his comeback. In his first game as a St. Louis Blue he shut out Los Angeles 6–0. He and Hall went on to win the Vezina Trophy and to produce the lowest goals-against average record of a Vezina winner in 13 years. Plante's average was 1.96, Hall's 2.17. Their combined total was 2.07.

Pat Hughes Snapped a Gretzky Record

"SURE, RECORDS ARE MEANT to be broken — but not that quickly" is what Wayne Gretzky might have said to Pat Hughes the night Hughes did the impossible. Gretzky, you see, had just established another in his amazing collection of NHL scoring records, and it was one that made him proud. As an Edmonton Oiler one night, with his team shorthanded, the Great One had slipped through the opposing team's power play and scored. Not once but twice — on the same shift. Two goals in 27 seconds while playing shorthanded is an amazing feat. No player in NHL history had ever come close to such a mark. Even Gretzky conceded: "That's a record that should last a long, long time."

A few nights later the Oilers again found themselves shorthanded. Helping to kill the penalty was forward Pat Hughes, a decent scorer but hardly in Gretzky's class when it came to scoring shorthanded goals or any other kind of goals. But Hughes broke away and lit the lamp with a surprise score. Moments later he did it again. To his and everyone else's astonishment, he had scored twice in 25 seconds while killing a penalty, and Gretzky's newly minted mark was shattered.

Wayne laughed about the oddity. "That's one of my records that didn't last too long," he told Hughes after the game.

But wait! Another Oiler, Esa Tikkanen, had a surprise up his sleeve. In the first period of a game against Toronto on November 12, 1988, he snapped in a pair of shorthanded goals in a mere 12 seconds, causing both Gretzky and Hughes to shake their heads in disbelief.

PART

OFF-ICE OVERSEERS AND PUNDITS

Cherry Calls Time-out to Sign Autographs

EVER HEAR OF AN NHL COACH calling a time-out in a game to sign autographs? Don Cherry did it on the night he coached the woeful Colorado Rockies to an upset victory over his former team, the Boston Bruins. It was December 2, 1979, and Cherry was itching for a win when he brought his Rockies into the Boston Garden for the first time since he was dismissed as the Bruins' coach in the off-season. Not only was he still miffed at Boston general manager Harry Sinden for firing him, he had just heard that two Boston players, Gilles Gilbert and John Wensink, had bad-mouthed him to the press.

"I can understand Gilbert criticizin' me," Cherry snorted to the reporters. "Did he tell you how I tried to start him five times last season and he came up with five different excuses why he couldn't play? And every time we'd go into Montreal he'd give me some excuse why he couldn't play there. It got to be a joke.

"And for Wensink to say I played favorites really disappoints me. He should get down on his knees every night and thank the Lord that I did play favorites, or he'd have been battin' his brains out in the International League."

So Cherry hungered for a victory over his former club that December night. He knew it was unlikely to happen. His Rockies had won just five of their 22 starts while the Bruins were on top of their division. For the occasion Cherry wore a three-piece ultraviolet velvet suit, one he had been planning to wear in the previous year's Stanley Cup finals. And would have if his team hadn't been ousted by Montreal in game seven of the semifinals — the series decided when Boston was caught with too many men on the ice.

But the Boston fans were quick to show Cherry he was missed and still loved, rising to give him a standing ovation when he took his place behind the visiting team's bench. As usual the Rockies got off to a sluggish start and fell behind 2–0. Then someone said, "Come on, guys, let's dig in and win this for Grapes." And they did, squeezing out a 5–3 victory, with the last shot hitting the empty Boston net. The most talked-about moment in the game came in the third period when Cherry called a time-out. His players gathered at the bench, but he discussed no strategy, offered no words of encouragement. To their amazement, and to the delight of everyone in the building, he turned his back on them and started signing autographs.

"It was just somethin' that happened," he told me later. "I didn't plan it. I wasn't tryin' to twist the knife in or nothin'. I was just tryin' to give my defensemen a rest. Then people started askin' me for my autograph, so I signed some things. You can bet my bosses in Colorado weren't too happy about that."

One of Cherry's supporters that night was D. Leo Monahan, a longtime Boston hockey writer. The following day he wrote: "Grapes couldn't have written a better script. The man may showboat a bit but he's a gem among his drab, colorless, cliché-speaking brethren. Hail, Don Cherry, hail."

Harry Neale Gets a Message from Gordie Howe

WHEN HARRY NEALE FIRST COACHED Gordie Howe, the hockey superstar was almost in his fifties, the oldest player in pro hockey. Harry had difficulty treating Howe like all the other players on the Hartford Whalers, some of whom were young enough to be Howe's sons. Hell, two of them were his sons.

Neale would set a curfew at 11:00 p.m. and tell his players, "You better be in your rooms, because I'll be checking on you."

At 11:00 p.m. he would make his rounds, and when he came to Howe's room, he would see the light under the door and hear the TV set. So he would say to himself, Gordie's obviously in there. I'm not going to disturb a hockey legend. I'll pass on to the next room.

One morning Howe took him aside and asked, "Harry, am I on this team or not?"

"Of course you're on the team. What do you mean?"

"You set a curfew and said you were going to check our rooms. I usually go to sleep about 10:30, and I keep waiting up for you, sometimes until 11:30, but you don't show up. You never do."

"Well, I . . ."

"Never mind that," Howe said. "If I'm on this team, I want to be treated like everybody else. Don't ever do that again."

Look, Up in the Sky, It's a Referee!

HALF A CENTURY AGO, when Frank Carlin managed the Montreal Royals hockey club, life on the road was full of surprises.

"We went into Boston once," Carlin told me, "and there didn't appear to be a referee for the game. There were two linesmen, but no ref. When I mentioned his absence to the linesmen, they just laughed and said, 'He's up there.' Then they pointed skyward. Sure enough, high over the ice, sitting in a gondola, was the referee. Somebody figured he'd have a better overall view of things if he was high over the ice in a kind of basket. I swear it was the only time I'd ever seen such a thing. So we played in the only game in which the referee was perched forty or fifty feet above the action. If he called a lousy penalty, the players below had nobody to argue with except for the linesmen. And all they said was, 'Don't tell us about it. He's the guy who made the call.' And they'd point skyward again."

Carlin recalled another time when his team went on a tour of Europe. "We arrived in Paris and some promoters wanted us to play on a tiny little ice surface located in a nightclub. It was the poorest excuse for a hockey rink I'd ever seen. So I turned down the offer. But we went to see a game played there and it was hilarious. The rink was surrounded by brass rails supporting red velvet curtains designed to keep the puck in play. Every time the puck flew through the curtains the referee dived in after it, often landing between some woman's legs. One lady spectator patted him on the head and said, 'Oh, you naughty boy!' Seems to me he spent most of the night diving through those curtains. He had a wonderful time."

Colorful, Controversial Conn Smythe

ON MARCH 15, 1932, during the first period of a Toronto–Boston game played in Boston, Leaf goalie Lorne Chabot tripped the Bruins' Cooney Weiland. Chabot was sent to the penalty box for two minutes, and three Leafs — Red Horner, Alex Levinsky, and King Clancy — took turns defending the goal. There was only one goalie per team in those days. All three failed their netminding test as the Bruins rattled in three goals. The penalty to Chabot infuriated Leaf manager Conn Smythe, and when referee Bill Stewart skated past the visitors' bench, Smythe reached out, grabbed him by the sweater, and refused to let go. Finally Charles Adams, the Bruins' president, with several policemen in tow, persuaded Smythe to release the referee and allow the game to continue.

When Toronto star Ace Bailey suffered a fractured skull after being upended by Boston's Eddie Shore at the Boston Garden in December 1933, Smythe was one of the first men on the scene. While rink attendants carried the stricken Bailey off on a stretcher, hundreds of fans left their seats and filled the corridors of the Boston Garden. When one Bruin fan refused to get out of Smythe's way, he punched the man and was promptly arrested and charged with assault. The charge was later withdrawn when the judge ruled that Smythe had acted under great stress.

41

During the 1936–37 season, Smythe accused
Montreal officials of a sneaky trick. He claimed that
an attempt had been made to slow down his fast
players by blunting the blades of their skates.
"Someone sneaked into our dressing room and
spread sand on the floor," was his accusation. General manager Tommy Gorman of the Maroons dismissed Smythe's charge as nonsense. "If there's
sand on the floor, Smythe must have brought it from
Toronto — from one of those sandpits he owns."

When the Toronto Maple Leafs invaded the Boston Garden for a game in January 1937, Smythe
appeared on the Toronto bench wearing a cutaway
evening jacket, striped trousers, spats, and a top
hat. His attire, he told reporters, was designed to
add some much-needed class to Boston hockey

*The Stanley Cup is presented to the Maple Leafs' Conn Smythe
(center) in 1942. At extreme left is coach Hap Day with star player
Syl Apps.* (Turofsky)

circles. The attendant publicity he received in the Boston papers pleased Smythe and infuriated his archrival, Boston GM Art Ross.

During the same season, when his Toronto club lost a game in New York, Smythe leaped over the boards and began a heated argument with the referee and the goal judge. When big Art Coulter of the Rangers skated in between Smythe and the officials, the diminutive Smythe threw a wild punch that caught Coulter right in the mouth.

At a Montreal–Toronto match in Maple Leaf Gardens, Smythe leaped into the penalty box to blister the ears of the Canadiens' player-coach Sylvio Mantha, who was serving a minor penalty. When referee Mike Rodden skated over to order Smythe out of the box, the Leaf owner grabbed Rodden by the sweater and wouldn't let go. During the struggle, Smythe took an usher's hat and slapped it on the struggling referee's head. Leaf coach Dick Irvin joined the fracas and belted Mantha. Then NHL president Frank Calder rushed to the scene, along with Ernest Savard, governor of the Canadiens. Fans gaped at the astonishing sight. There was the NHL president and two of his governors, plus a coach and a player-coach, all pushing, shoving, and shouting in the penalty box.

One year Smythe accused the Toronto sportswriters of not telling the truth. As a result, he made the newspapers pay to have their reporters attend Leaf games. "Newspapermen are crooks!" he declared. "They are glad to take my money, glad to put my ads in their papers, glad to take my free seats to the games. And then they don't write the truth! From now on let them pay to get into Leaf games."

On the eve of a Toronto–Boston game in Boston,

Smythe bought advertising space in all the Boston papers. Addressed to the Bruin fans, it read: "If you're tired of what you've been looking at lately, the sleep-producing hockey as played by the Boston hockey club, come out tonight and see a decent team play the game the way it should be played."

The Bruins' Art Ross was furious with Smythe and demanded the NHL censure him. The league governors met in time and decided to censure both Smythe and Ross for their constant bickering.

Wrong Man, Wrong Time, Wrong Place

REMEMBER NED HARKNESS? He was the coach and later general manager of the Detroit Red Wings for a couple of seasons in the seventies. He had made his reputation in U.S. college hockey and become the first man to jump from campus rinks to coach in the pros, only to fall flat on his tush in Motor City.

Was it Ned's rah-rah approach, treating the pros like college kids, that killed his chances for success in Detroit? Or was Fred Shero right when he said, "Harkness had many things going for him, but hockey players and club owners are afraid of outsiders. They're afraid of shocks."

There was no question that Harkness jolted the Wings right from day one. At training camp he introduced new methods, such as a novel forechecking system and some interesting conditioning drills. His chalk talks annoyed the veterans, who complained about being treated like "collegians."

Gordie Howe, Alex Delvecchio, and Frank Mahovlich all got their digs in.

Harkness fought back, pointing the finger at general manager Sid Abel. He complained about the complacency within the organization. He griped about the lack of scouting reports and was annoyed when Abel told him, "Don't worry, Ned. Things will work out."

Eventually Abel, irritated by the criticism, delivered an ultimatum to team owner Bruce Norris. "Either Harkness goes or I go."

"We're going to miss you, Sid," Norris replied. "I'm sticking with Harkness."

But the veteran players sided with Abel. Like them, he was old school. The Red Wings drew up a petition. If Harkness wasn't fired, they would refuse to play. Gordie Howe was chosen to hand Bruce Norris the edict. When he saw it, Norris was shocked.

Still he backed Harkness and asked him to be both coach and general manager. But Harkness was ready to throw in the towel as coach. He knew it was hopeless. The Wings were never going to play Harkness-style hockey. He resigned and accepted Abel's old job as the Wings' general manager.

The poisonous stories spread about Harkness by the players and passed along to the press were translated into animosity by the fans. His car windows were broken and his home was splattered with eggs. One fan attacked him physically, while others sent him death threats. Before long, bags of hate mail streamed into the Red Wings' offices.

By February 1974 the situation had become intolerable. When Harkness resigned from the organization, he made no explanation, only saying, "I guess

I was the wrong man, with the wrong team, at the wrong time."

I knew Ned Harkness long before he reached the NHL. Our St. Lawrence University hockey teams often played against his Rensselaer Polytechnic Institute (RPI) squads in the fifties. Harkness was the greatest college hockey coach I had ever seen. We knew him as the Miracle Man at RPI for his ability to take teams with little depth right to the heights. In 1954 his RPI team had two lines, a pair of defensemen, and a goalie. He guided it past powerful Michigan and Minnesota to win the NCAA title at Colorado Springs. His record at RPI was 187–90–7, despite the fact that he never had the luxury of coaching talent-laden teams.

In the 1960s he moved on to Cornell and molded a hockey powerhouse. His record there was truly astonishing — 163–27–2. And that was in his first three years on the job before he was able to stock his teams with players he had recruited personally. From 1967 to 1970 Cornell captured two national titles, four straight ECAC crowns, and five straight Ivy League championships. One of his stars was goalie Ken Dryden, who played in only three losing games during his college career. During one stretch in 1970, Cornell went a record 29 games without a loss.

After the disaster in Detroit, Harkness embarked on a program to bring top college hockey to Union College in Schenectady, New York. He began with no arena and no team, and when he was able to ice a team of freshmen and sophomores, he quickly ran up a record of 48–6–2 against varsity competition. He resigned in 1978, stating, "I'm a hockey coach, not a politician," a remark aimed at college administrators who were said to be harassing him.

Buying a Time-out . . . with Cash

DURING THE 1986 STANLEY CUP PLAYOFFS, St. Louis coach Jacques Demers tried to buy a little time for his team. And he was brought up to believe that whenever you buy something, you are expected to pay for it. So whenever he needed a little extra time to give his players a breather, he tossed some pennies onto the ice.

When warned by the referee not to do it again, Demers said, "It's true. I got caught. But I'm not the first coach to get a few extra seconds that way. I've seen tape tossed out there, a player's mouth guard dropped over the boards, lots of things."

When a reporter asked him how he would have felt if a security man had tossed him out of the rink for throwing objects onto the ice, he replied, "I never thought of that. I would have been very embarrassed."

Hot Words Between Coach and Player

SELDOM HAVE I WITNESSED the degree of hostility that existed between Miroslav Frycer and his coach John Brophy when both were on the Toronto Maple Leaf payroll. They despised each other over the course of two seasons, and both were elated when Frycer was traded to Detroit (for Darren Veitch) in June 1988.

Neither could put their animosity to rest, and their quotes about each other made lively reading.

"I hate Brophy," Frycer said after he led his new team to an 8–2 win over the Leafs at Maple Leaf Gardens. "If the two goals I scored tonight help to get him fired, that's good. He deserves to be fired. I even gave him the finger after the game. He's a bad person. He's the worst human being I ever met, including anyone I ever met in Czechoslovakia. I met a lot of Communists there, and they were pleasant compared to him."

Over to you, John.

"Frycer? I'm sick and tired of that Communist. He sneaked out through a hole in a wire fence someplace and now he shoots his mouth off. It's pretty easy to join a club [Detroit] that's set. What did he do in his years here? How many games did he play here the last two years between being drunk and being arrested?"

Brophy was referring to a brief jail sentence for drunken driving that Frycer served the previous summer.

A few days after the Frycer–Brophy tirades, Brophy was canned by the Leafs. His two-year record at the helm was 54–111–18. Frycer must have enjoyed a long laugh when he heard the news.

But Brophy had reason to laugh two weeks later. Detroit traded Frycer to Edmonton for next to nothing — a 10th-round draft choice. The Wings accused him of being a bad influence on Czechoslovakian countryman Petr Klima. "Frycer will never wear a Detroit uniform again," coach Jacques Demers said.

Breaking Up Is Not Hard to Do

HOCKEY BROADCASTERS HAVE their moments. I know. I have been one. One day I asked Toronto Maple Leaf announcer Joe Bowen and his then partner Bill Watters if there was one incident they could recall that really cracked them up.

Bowen says, "Oh, yeah, the Leafs are playing in Edmonton one night and the club had just signed, at great expense, that noted plumber from Czechoslovakia, Miroslav Ihnacak. Lasted half a season. Anyway, the kid had just arrived and it was his second or third game and he wants to make an impression. So he takes a run at Mark Messier who's in along the boards with his big elbow stuck out like this [demonstrates]. Now here comes this rookie from across the rink and rams his nose right into Messier's elbow. What a smack when he hit! Well, down he goes and Billy and I start to laugh. It was hilarious. Poor Ihnacak is lying there quivering, and there's blood all over the place and we're hysterical. Then Billy says, 'I think the poor guy's got CCM tattooed on his bugle.'

"Well, that did it. Now we're really laughing. Here they're scraping poor Ihnacak off the ice and we're busting our guts in the booth. Then the game is under way, and I still can't control the laughter, so I went to a commercial — right in the middle of the play. I'd never done that before, but I had to. Luckily no goals were scored while we were away. And the game was on radio, not TV, so nobody said anything or noticed anything except maybe they thought a couple of damn hyenas were calling the play."

Bill Watters adds, "We were under control when we came back from the commercial, and everything was rolling along just fine . . . until we saw Ihnacak jump back onto the ice . . ."

"That's when we lost it again," Bowen interjects. "We both thought of Ihnacak taking dead aim on Messier's elbow, running right at it from 50 feet, and going down like a sack of wheat, so we started cackling and howling again. I can't believe we got through the rest of that period."

An Embarrassing Moment for Grapes

DON CHERRY WOULD PROBABLY like to forget the following incident. During a playoff series between the the Los Angeles Kings and the Edmonton Oilers, Don found himself in the Los Angeles airport waiting for a flight. Across the airport waiting room he spotted a familiar figure, that of Brant Heywood, the *Hockey Night in Canada* isolation director. Heywood was bending over to tie an errant shoelace. Approaching his friend from behind, Cherry gave Heywood a friendly pat on the bum. But the man who straightened up, the man who turned and gave Cherry a withering look, didn't look like Heywood one bit. "Do you meet many men this way?" he asked Cherry before he hurried away.

The younger Don Cherry in his coaching days, dapper as ever in plaid.

(Steve Babineau)

A Message for the King

WHEN KING CLANCY RETIRED as a hockey player, he turned to refereeing. One day he told me about a game he worked in New York.

"It was during World War II and some soldiers were on hand for the opening ceremonies. It was very dramatic the way they dimmed the lights as everybody stood for *The Star-Spangled Banner.* Then the soldiers raised their rifles and prepared to fire a volley. It was a solemn moment and a hush fell over the crowd. Then, way up in the top balcony, some leather-lunged fan bellowed out, 'When you get through with all that — shoot Clancy!'"

51

Ballard Fires Neilson, or Does He?

ON MARCH 1, 1979, the struggling Maple Leafs met the Montreal Canadiens at the Forum. It was a big game for Toronto coach Roger Neilson. Prior to the match, his boss, 75-year-old Harold Ballard, told reporters, "Neilson will be gone . . . fired if the Leafs don't win."

Late in the game, with Toronto trailing 2–1, Ballard told Dick Beddoes, then a member of our telecast crew, that Neilson indeed was toast. The dismissal of Neilson, a very popular guy, made headlines everywhere. I ran into the coach in a Toronto restaurant the next day and commiserated with him. He, in turn, said he was confused because he hadn't heard anything yet from Ballard. The Leaf players, meanwhile, led by Tiger Williams and Darryl Sittler, huddled with Ballard and pleaded with him to bring Roger back. There was even a rumor that they might refuse to take the ice for their next home game if Roger wasn't behind the bench.

By Saturday Ballard had either reconsidered or he couldn't find a competent replacement for Neilson. He talked to John McLellan about taking over, but McLellan said he wanted no part of the assignment. So Ballard called Neilson in and rehired him. But the Leaf boss, always the showman, kept the move a secret. Ballard even suggested that Neilson wear a paper bag over his head when he took his place behind the Leaf bench that night. It would be quite a sensation, especially since the game was on *Hockey Night in Canada*.

Neilson wisely decided against the paper bag suggestion, and when he did make his appearance, the ovation he received was tremendous. Alas, his return was short-lived. A few weeks later Ballard decided not to renew his contract.

"They Asked Me to Coach"

IN ALL THE CONFUSION SURROUNDING the firing and rehiring of Toronto coach Roger Neilson in March 1979, I wound up with a great deal of egg on my face.

Prior to Neilson's surprising return — without a bag over his head — for the Saturday night game at Maple Leaf Gardens following his "dismissal" in Montreal, I tried frantically to learn the identity of the man Ballard had selected to replace him as Leaf coach. As the color commentator on the telecast, it was important that I say something about the new coach at the beginning of the program.

Minutes before game time, seeking the latest developments, I dashed into the Leaf front office where I encountered head scout Gerry McNamara. "Help me out, Gerry," I pleaded. "We're going coast-to-coast in a few minutes and I've got to know who's coaching tonight."

"You've come to the right place," he said. "They've asked me to coach tonight."

"That's all I need to know. Thanks, Gerry."

I raced to the gondola and moments later announced to a huge television audience that Gerry McNamara would be the new Leaf coach. At precisely that moment Roger Neilson emerged from the Leaf dressing room and strolled to the Leaf bench while the crowd roared its approval.

I was dumbfounded. Where was McNamara? Why

had he lied to me about taking over as coach? Was he deliberately trying to make me look like a buffoon?

On Monday morning I walked into McNamara's office and confronted him. "Gerry, why did you lie to me on Saturday night?" I asked him, my collar still warm.

"But I didn't lie to you," he replied calmly. "I told you on Saturday that they had asked me to coach. I didn't say I would be coach. There's a difference, you know."

Perhaps there was a difference . . . a small one. But there was no doubt he had led me to believe he would be Neilson's replacement. Hence the egg all over my face.

"Wipe That Tan Off, Miller!"

BOSTON COACH DON CHERRY was preparing his Bruins for a playoff series with Montreal one year. After a morning workout in Boston, the team reassembled later that day for the bus ride to the airport and the flight to Montreal. The weather had turned exceptionally balmy in Boston, and forward Bobby Miller had taken advantage of the soaring temperature to lie out in the sun for a couple of hours. The result — a beautiful tan. When Miller boarded the bus, Cherry had a fit.

"Look at you, Miller," he snorted. "You're all brown, for God's sake. You've got a tan. The rest of us is white and you've got a tan."

As Miller scurried down the aisle of the bus, Cherry gave him a parting shot. "I'm tellin' you right now, Miller. Get rid of it!"

The Scuttling of "Showdown"

"**S**HOWDOWN," A CREATION of TV producer Paul Palmer, was one of the most popular intermission segments we ever featured on *Hockey Night in Canada*. It was also seen on the NBC hockey telecasts in the 1970s. The show was produced during the off-season and took about four days to complete. Fans loved it, and the NHL stars selected for the competition enjoyed matching their skills against their peers.

Palmer had received permission from the NHL Players' Association to produce the show. It had been sanctioned by the member clubs and the NHL itself. While most hockey men agreed that the show was a good idea, a small number objected. Buffalo general manager Punch Imlach and Leaf owner Harold Ballard were reluctant to let their players participate. Imlach talked Danny Gare and Gilbert Perreault out of competing one year, and Ballard was furious when Borje Salming was slightly injured during one of the events.

There was a major confrontation in 1979. Leaf stars Mike Palmateer and Darryl Sittler agreed to take part in a new edition of "Showdown." By then Punch Imlach, fired by the Sabres, had resurfaced as the Toronto general manager, and he put his foot down. His star players would not be allowed to appear in "Showdown." If Palmer wanted Leaf representation, he could have Gord McRae and Paul Gardner, two journeyman players. But Sittler and Palmateer would not be available.

When Al Eagleson, Sittler's agent, argued vehemently with Imlach over this issue, the Leafs hired a lawyer and sought an injunction to prevent the two players from taking part. But a justice of the Ontario Supreme Court ruled against the Leafs. Sittler and Palmateer were free to participate in "Showdown." But Imlach and Ballard weren't through yet. In his television contract Ballard had the right to approve the intermission content on Maple Leaf telecasts, and he promptly blackballed "Showdown." There was no recourse this time, no argument. Without the huge Toronto market "Showdown" was over, never to be seen again. Ballard and Imlach were the winners, the players and viewers the losers.

Storey Turns Tattletale

RED STOREY, the former NHL referee and popular after-dinner speaker, likes to tell this story about his old pal, linesman George Hayes. If Hall of Famer Hayes were alive today, he would grumble, "Damn that Storey. He was never supposed to mention what happened. He promised. The guy's nothin' but a tattletale."

Hayes was a thrifty kind of guy, and when he traveled by train to his various NHL assignments, he often packed a lunch to carry aboard. Storey was visiting Hayes at his Ingersoll, Ontario, home one day and they were getting ready to leave for a game in Detroit. In the Hayes kitchen Storey noticed a couple of empty cans of dog food.

"George, I didn't know you had a dog," he said.

Hayes turned beet-red. "I don't. Red, you won't believe it, but I was shopping the other day and I thought I was buying some tins of tuna. But I made a mistake and bought dog food instead. I didn't notice the difference, and on my last road trip I made tuna fish sandwiches — with the dog food. Unbelievable! I thought there was something funny about the way they tasted. But, listen, you gotta promise me you won't breathe a word of this to anybody."

Laughing so hard he could barely answer, Red said, "Sure, George, sure. I promise. Your secret's safe with me."

They went on to Detroit, and Red was still chuckling over the dog food story. He was bursting to share it with somebody. As soon as the warm-up was over and the anthem was played, he skated over to Gordie Howe and Bill Gadsby and told them about Hayes eating the dog food sandwiches.

The two Red Wings knew what to do. Gadsby

A classic confrontation: referee Red Storey and tough guy Red Wing Ted Lindsay exchange words. (David Bier)

skated up close to Hayes and started howling like a dog. Howe came along and added a few "Woof, woofs," then attempted to pat Hayes on the head. After that Howe and Gadsby couldn't stop laughing.

But Hayes didn't think it was funny. Fuming, he skated up to Storey and said, "You son of a bitch. You told those guys, didn't you? And you promised you wouldn't."

Storey didn't answer. He was too busy getting set to drop the puck for the opening face-off.

A Gift for Grapes

WHEN DON "GRAPES" CHERRY coached the Boston Bruins, he received an unusual gift one year at the team's annual Christmas party. Knowing of Cherry's love for animals, particularly dogs, they tried to find out what kind of canine Grapes didn't like.

"I love all dogs," he told them, "especially bull terriers like my pal Blue. They're the greatest. But if you really want to know a dog I can't stand, it's those Yorkies [Yorkshire terrier]. They're too small and too yappy. Can't stand small, yappy dogs or small, yappy players."

So what did the Bruins give their coach at the Christmas party? A tiny purebred Yorkshire terrier puppy worth about $500. Cherry brought it home, and his daughter Cindy promptly fell in love with it. But his dog Blue hated the pup and threatened to eat it alive. Obviously it had to go. Ken Hodge of the Bruins volunteered to take it, so it moved to a good home. But the rest of the Bruins were a little upset.

They had raised $500 to buy a dog for Cherry — and Ken Hodge got to keep it.

Scotty Bowman Scored the First Penalty Shot Goal

I AM COMPELLED TO BEGIN my story about Ralph "Scotty" Bowman with the answer to a question often asked. Did Scotty Bowman, the famous hockey coach, really score the first penalty shot goal in the NHL?

The answer, of course, is no, not that Scotty Bowman.

William Scott Bowman, the coach, wasn't born yet when Ralph "Scotty" Bowman, a defenseman with the old St. Louis Eagles, created hockey history on November 13, 1934.

"The referee called a penalty shot for some reason," Bowman told Randy Schultz of the *The Hockey News* some time ago. "Because the penalty shot was a new feature to hockey, the players stood around waiting for some direction.

"Our coach, Eddie Gerard, selected me to take the shot. I don't know why. I wasn't known to be much of a scorer. [Bowman scored eight goals in a seven-year NHL career.]

"The ref placed the puck in a big circle and told me I had a choice of shooting it from a standing position or shooting it on the run. I chose to shoot it on the run, and it sailed past goalie Alex Connell's leg and into the net. It's a goal I'll never forget, even though a lot of fans think it was Bowman the coach who scored that night."

PART

BATTLERS AND WARRIORS

Don Cherry's Memories of Eddie Shore

DON CHERRY, hockey's most colorful hockey commentator, played defense for Springfield of the American Hockey League for four seasons. This gave him plenty of opportunity to observe the bizarre behavior of owner-manager-coach Eddie Shore. Among Cherry's observations:

- The Springfield players were ordered by Shore never to tip a cabdriver more than 15 cents. Soon there wasn't a driver in the city who would pick up anyone who even resembled a hockey player.
- Shore never balked at adding bonus clauses to a player's contract, but there always seemed to be a catch. For example, he would grant a player a handsome bonus for scoring 30 goals. But the player, when he reached 29 goals, was likely to find himself riding the bench for the rest of the season.
- Shore's "Black Aces" were players who had somehow crossed him or enraged him. They practiced with his team but seldom played. The Black Aces were required to paint the arena seats, sell programs at games, make popcorn, and blow up balloons for special events.
- In Shore's opinion, if a referee made a glaring mistake, he might find himself locked in or out of the officials' dressing room. Shore

had the key to the padlock on the door. If Shore felt the official was truly inept, he would denounce the arbiter over the arena public-address system.

- While Shore was giving his players an on-ice lecture at practice one day, Cherry made the mistake of looking up at the clock. Cherry's glance upward infuriated Shore, and the punishment he meted out was severe. Cherry was forced to skate laps around the rink for the next four and a half hours — in the dark. Shore never kept the arena lights on if there was no good reason for doing so.
- Shore often climbed a high platform on wheels to change light bulbs over the ice

in the arena. One of his serfs (Black Aces) would be recruited to move the platform from spot to spot as Shore shouted directions from above. One day Ken Schinkel pushed the platform from under Shore's body, leaving him dangling by his arms from a girder. If Schinkel expected to hear screams of fear or outrage from his boss, he was mistaken. Shore looked down and calmly ordered Schinkel to "get that platform under my feet and be quick about it." Schinkel did, knowing full well that his little prank would keep him with the Black Aces for a long time to come.

- During the playoffs one season, Shore issued invitations to the wives of the Springfield players, asking them if they could gather at the arena one night between games. The wives assumed the owner-coach was planning a little party for the team, and they decided to dress for the occasion. At the arena on the appointed night the ladies were ushered into the Springfield dressing room, which reeked of liniment and smelly underwear. Shore came in and addressed the group. "Ladies, we're in a bit of a slump, and you're partly responsible. You're giving your husbands too much sex. Please give it up until the season is over." Then the wives were dismissed. In leaving, one of them was heard to say, "I wouldn't have minded so much if what he had said was true. But it's certainly not in our case."

In his book *Grapes,* Cherry points out that Shore was a "masterful teacher and from one of his championship teams no less than 14 players went on to become professional coaches."

Hunter Serves Long, Costly Suspension

IT HAPPENED DURING THE FINAL GAME of the Islanders–Capitals playoff series in 1993 in the Patrick Division semifinals. Pierre Turgeon, the Isles' leading scorer, raised his arms to celebrate a goal, and that was the last thing he remembered. He was blindsided by a frustrated Dale Hunter of the Caps and suffered a separated shoulder and a concussion.

NHL commissioner Gary Bettman stepped in and nailed Hunter with a 21-game suspension, the second longest punishment for an on-ice incident in league history. The Capitals were also fined $150,000.

"I picked 21 games because it happened to be the maximum number of playoff games the Islanders could be without Turgeon," Bettman said.

Hunter claimed he didn't know a goal had been scored when he hit Turgeon and that he was merely finishing his check. But video evidence showed him slamming into the Islander player four or five seconds after the scoring play.

The suspension, which prohibited Hunter from taking part in Washington's training camp prior to the 1993–94 season and kept him out of the first 21 regular season games, cost the player approximately $150,000 in lost salary.

Bobby Hull in Hair-raising Encounter

DAVE HANSON IS MORE FAMOUS for a role he played in the movie *Slapshot* than for anything he did on the ice in the NHL or the WHA. But he does recall an encounter with Bobby Hull in Winnipeg one night that brought him instant notoriety. Here is how Hanson remembers it.

"When I was in the WHA with Birmingham, I didn't have a lot of talent, but I wanted to impress some people. We were playing Winnipeg one night and I was on defense. I figured the fastest way to make a name for myself was to step into Bobby Hull and put him on his back.

"Well, Bobby came flying down the wing and I stepped into him and he flattened me. He knocked me right on my ass and skated over my face, leaving me gasping and humiliated. My pride was hurt and I made up my mind that the next time he came in on me I was going to be better prepared. I'd really get him.

"He came down again and I got my elbows up and roughed him, which he didn't take kindly to. So we dropped the gloves and started flailing away at each other. Then, to my amazement, I felt something soft. I had a full head of hair in my hands! I looked down and discovered I was holding Bobby's wig. I said, 'Oh, shit!' and threw the hairpiece out in the middle of the ice. Bobby just stood there completely bald, and the fans were as stunned as he was. It was as if the air had been sucked out of the building. You could hear a pin drop. I got fifteen minutes in penalties, and Bobby didn't get anything.

"The next day in the paper there was a huge picture of Ulf Nilsson, Bobby's linemate, looking down at this wig on the ice. You should have seen the headlines. All the Hull fans wanted to kill me. Reporters wrote things like: 'Some idiot out of nowhere embarrassed the Golden Jet' and 'Is nothing sacred? It's like painting a mustache on the *Mona Lisa*.' Radio stations started calling me for open-line interviews, asking things like 'Why would you do such a thing?' I must say Bobby Hull took it well. After it happened, he skated off to the dressing room and put on a helmet. When he came back, I went over to him and apologized. I really felt terrible. He said, 'Aw, don't worry about it, kid.' He took it in stride."

The NHL's Longest Suspension

MOST NEWSPAPERS and *The Hockey News* called Dale Hunter's 21-game suspension in 1993 "the longest in league history for an on-ice incident." Somehow they overlooked the lifetime suspension doled out to Billy Couture (often called Coutu) during the 1927 playoffs.

Couture, one of the meanest, toughest defensemen ever to terrorize the NHL, was a member of the Boston Bruins when he was banned forever by NHL president Frank Calder. During a brawl involving several players on the Bruins and the Ottawa Senators, Couture smashed referee Gerry Laflamme in the face. Calder banned him for life, a suspension that was lifted five years later — too late for Couture to return to the NHL.

Tiger Gets His Favorite Number

WHEN TIGER WILLIAMS was traded from Toronto to Vancouver in 1980, he discovered that his favorite jersey number — 22 — was being worn by the Canucks' Bob Manno. In the dressing room Tiger wasn't shy about speaking up. "Hey, Bob," he said, "I'll give you 10 grand if you'll let me have your number."

Manno looked at Tiger and said, "Nah, I don't think so."

Two weeks later Manno was dispatched to the minor leagues, never to return. When he turned in his jersey with the big 22 on the back, Tiger was there to collect it.

"And it didn't cost me a penny," Tiger said.

Rehashing an Old Feud

OLD HOCKEY PLAYERS, like elephants, never forget. In 1963 at a B'nai B'rith banquet in Boston several members of the Hockey Hall of Fame were invited as honored guests. Prior to the dinner, the old-timers gathered in a hotel suite, as was the custom at such gatherings, to reminisce and rehash stories from their athletic youth.

Two of the former greats, Aurel Joliat and Punch Broadbent, recalled a fistfight they had been in 40 years earlier during a game between the Montreal Canadiens and the Ottawa Senators. Joliat's version of the fight differed somewhat from Broadbent's. Harsh words were exchanged, voices were raised,

69

insults exchanged, and punches filled the air. There they were, two men in their sixties, rolling around on the floor, swearing, grunting, and flailing away at each other.

In order to restore order and keep the peace, the two out-of-breath combatants were led to their rooms and locked in until they cooled off.

Randy's One-man Riot

ON MARCH 11, 1979, at the Philadelphia Spectrum, Randy Holt of the Los Angeles Kings declared a one-man war against the Flyers' Frank Bathe. Holt racked up nine penalties totaling an NHL-record 67 minutes. He collected one minor, three majors, two 10-minute misconducts, and three game misconducts — all in the first period. Bathe, the Flyer who scrapped with Holt several times in the opening period, finished the game with 55 penalty minutes, the second highest single-game total ever. While Holt still holds the single-game record for penalty minutes, he failed to hold on to his nine-penalty record. On March 31, 1991, Chris Nilan, then with the Boston Bruins, took 10 penalties in a game against Hartford.

The Night Clancy Goaded Shore

IN THE THIRTIES King Clancy of the Leafs and Eddie Shore of the Bruins were tops among NHL defensemen. Both were fierce competitors, and almost every time they met there were fireworks.

During one playoff series, a two-game, total-goals-to-count affair, the Bruins shut out the Leafs 3–0 on home ice and were heavily favored to advance when the teams met in game two at Maple Leaf Gardens. Many years ago, when I helped King chronicle his memoirs for the book *Clancy*, he recalled the bizarre ending to that story.

"We played terrible hockey in that first game in Boston, and I was ready to try anything to help us win that second match. I made up my mind to needle Shore if the opportunity came up, 'cause he had such a short fuse. I even told my mates when we left the dressing room that night, 'I got Shore in my hip pocket.'

"Well, Boston picked up where they left off and scored the first goal to take a four-goal lead in the series. Then Shore took a penalty, and while he was cooling off, I scored one and Conacher added another, cutting the margin in half. Then Red Horner scored a big goal for us, and Shore was livid, claiming Horner was in the crease on the play. That's when I skated over to Shore and said, 'That was a raw decision, Eddie. Of course, Horner was in the crease. The referee robbed you on that one.'

"Well, Shore blew his stack. He grabbed the puck and whipped it at referee Odie Cleghorn, hitting him in the back. Cleghorn spun around and gave Shore a 10-minute misconduct, and that was the turning point. We scored three quick goals while he was off and rolled to an 8–3 victory. Won the round eight goals to six. Shore never did forgive me for goading him into that penalty that night."

Linesman Hayes Was a Rebel

THEY FOUND A PLACE for the late George Hayes in the Hockey Hall of Fame a few years ago, and about time, too. Not only was Hayes one of the most colorful officials ever to skate around NHL rinks, he was one of the most controversial. He was a very large thorn in the side of his bosses — league president Clarence Campbell and referee-in-chief Carl Voss.

"I never had any use for Campbell from the first time I met the man," Hayes once told me. "He was the worst referee the league ever had. His problem was he was overeducated, being a Rhodes scholar and a war crimes prosecutor."

Hayes wouldn't even speak to Voss if he could avoid it. Voss had fined Hayes $50 one time for not

Hall of Fame linesman George Hayes (center) tries to break up a brawl between the Canadiens and the Bruins. (Hockey Hall of Fame)

shaving on a game day, and Hayes deeply resented this show of authority. He hated even more the loss of the $50, for he was notoriously tight with a buck.

He and Voss communicated by letter or memo. "One year I spoke to Voss only once. He interrupted a conversation I was having with Mr. Campbell at Maple Leaf Gardens one night, so I told him to shut up. He did and walked away."

What was the conversation with Campbell about?

"I forget, but he was probably making some dirty, sarcastic remark about my activities away from the rink."

Hayes loved to indulge in hockey's nastiest job — breaking up fights. He had the strength for it and knew something about fighting from his rebellious youth. He gave up hockey as a player when he couldn't stay out of the penalty box, and he once threw a fan over a fence for calling him a dirty name. Before he joined the NHL he was suspended for life from all organized sport for starting a riot during a ball game between two Ontario teams, Aylmer and Tillsonburg. The Ontario Provincial Police had to move in and break that one up.

One year Hayes and Campbell clashed over the issue of a life insurance program for NHL officials. Campbell recommended the program; Hayes was the only official who rejected it.

"I have no use for insurance of any kind, and I'm not paying $60 bucks for something I don't want," he told Campbell.

But the next season Hayes noticed a $60 deduction had been taken from his pay — for insurance.

"The buggers made a change in the contracts and I hadn't noticed it," he fumed. "They made insurance compulsory. Sixty bucks down the drain. Well,

I fixed them. I listed my dog Pete as my beneficiary. If I die, old Pete's going to be $20,000 richer."

Brother Flattens Brother

WHEN TIGER WILLIAMS, former NHL tough guy, was growing up in Weyburn, Saskatchewan, he developed a dislike for referees. His brother Len, who made a few bucks as an official, was no exception.

At the dinner table one day Tiger said to his brother, "Listen, Len, I'm playing a game tonight and I hear you're going to be the referee. I'm warning you right now. If you give me a penalty tonight, I'm going to pop you one."

But Len, like Tiger, wasn't easily intimidated. Sure enough, the game that night was barely under way when Len caught Tiger breaking a rule. He blew his whistle and waved him to the box. En route Tiger flattened his brother, just as he had promised.

The 80-second Game

WHEN JOHN BROPHY PLAYED for the Long Island Ducks in the old Eastern Hockey League, he teamed up on defense with Don Perry. Both men were tough and mean, the most feared combination on the circuit. They were so intimidating that one game they played in lasted a mere 80 seconds. The New Haven Blades were the opponents, and when Brophy and Perry clobbered a couple of Blades on the very first shift, that was enough. The Blades left the ice, put on their street clothes, and went home. Al Baron, owner of the Ducks, rushed to the visitors' dressing room and offered each player $100 to go back on the ice. To a man they replied, "No thanks, Al, not with those two crazies out there."

Williams and O'Reilly Share a Secret

IN HIS BOOK *Tiger: A Hockey Story,* Dave Williams recalls the night in Boston when Terry O'Reilly may have saved his life. In a previous game between the Leafs and the Bruins, Williams had nailed Boston's ace defenseman Bobby Orr with a tremendous body check.

In the return match at the Boston Garden, the Bruin enforcers were waiting for him, looking for revenge. Seconds after the opening face-off, Terry O'Reilly and Williams began throwing punches. They fought once, twice, three times, and in between the battles Tiger took a run at every Bruin who ventured down his wing. Eventually two of the toughest Bruins cornered him. O'Reilly threw him to the ice, and Wayne Cashman stood by, hoping to get his licks in. In the scuffle O'Reilly put a headlock on Williams, and that was when (according to Tiger) Cashman kicked him in the head. The skate blade sliced through his helmet and opened a cut that required six stitches.

O'Reilly reacted instantly. He whispered in Tiger's ear, "Put your head under my body and I'll shield you from Cashman." And Tiger took the advice. Another kick from Cashman and Tiger might have been seriously injured.

"From then on," Tiger said, "I always played O'Reilly

differently. I never elbowed him or gave him a cheap shot.

"You may wonder why O'Reilly didn't tell Cashman, 'Lay off, Cash. Don't be kicking a guy.' But that would have involved loss of face. Cashman might have told the other Bruins, 'O'Reilly's turned into a wimp.' So what happened became our little secret, O'Reilly's and mine. He didn't tell his mates and I didn't tell mine."

Paiement Pays for Polonich Pasting

DENIS POLONICH WAS a scrappy forward for Detroit. Wilf Paiement was a top scorer with the Colorado Rockies. Unfortunately they collided one night in a game during the 1978–79 season, and tempers flared. The sticks came up, and Paiement, wielding his like a baseball bat, struck Polonich in the face, resulting in severe facial injuries. Polonich sued, and in the landmark case that followed, Polonich won a civil action against Paiement. Under the terms of the settlement he agreed to accept over $1 million to be paid over the next two decades.

Little Camille Chases a Fan

THE 1959–60 SEASON was a pathetic one for the New York Rangers. They were submerged in last place and their playoff hopes were nil. But they earned no sympathy from some lunatic fans in Detroit one night. After they struggled to earn a single point in a 2–2 tie with the Red Wings, they were coming off the ice when they were pelted with an unusual amount of debris. Programs, popcorn boxes, wads of gum, shoe rubbers — they dodged it all. As they entered the corridor leading to their dressing room, little Camille Henry slipped on a program and fell, dropping his hockey stick.

A fan named Eric Steiner, a 37-year-old salesman, was standing nearby. He swooped in and grabbed the stick. Henry reached out to pull it back when Steiner smacked him acrross the face with the blade of the stick, opening up a wound under one eye that later required several stitches.

When Steiner saw the blood and the furious look on Henry's face, he took off and dashed out the nearest exit. Henry, the smallest player in the NHL, leaped up and ran after him. Out of the arena and down the street they raced, sparks flying from Henry's skates. Within a block he tackled the man and held him down until police arrived.

Arrested and charged with assault, Steiner's excuse was that he simply lost his head. Henry got his stick back and retraced his steps to the arena. Along the way fans leaving the game gaped at the sight of a New York Ranger, blood streaming from his face, clutching a stick under his arm, and clomping along in full hockey gear, including his skates.

Shack Loads His Gun, Shoots, and Scores

FORMER BUFFALO SABRE MIKE BYERS recalls playing on a line with Eddie "The Entertainer" Shack one night in Buffalo.

"We were waiting for the face-off in the other team's zone, and just before the official dropped the puck, Shack yells, 'Hold on a minute!' We all look over at him, and he's taking his hockey stick, turning it around, and cocking it like a rifle. Then he put the stick back in its original position and nodded, indicating he was ready for the face-off.

"Wouldn't you know, when the puck was dropped, it came right back to Shack and he snapped it into the net for a goal. Later I heard him tell reporters he stopped the game because his 'gun' was out of bullets. I'll say this, he picked a great time to reload."

Another First for Dino

ON AUGUST 24, 1988, winger Dino Ciccarelli, then with the Minnesota North Stars, became the first NHL player to receive a jail term for attacking a rival player on the ice. Judge Sydney Harris of Toronto sentenced Ciccarelli to 24 hours in jail and fined him $1,000 for clouting Toronto defenseman Luke Richardson twice with his stick (over the head) and punching him in the mouth during a game in January. Released after a two-hour stint behind bars, Ciccarelli called the verdict "utterly ridiculous." Asked to describe his stay in the slammer, he said, "The first thing I saw was a big fat cop eating a jelly doughnut. Then I stood around signing autographs for the other poor guys in there."

The Day Eddie Shack
Went Deaf

IN THE SIXTIES the Toronto Maple Leafs journeyed to Peterborough, Ontario, for their training camp. Right winger Eddie Shack, always at loggerheads with general manager-coach Punch Imlach, hadn't signed a contract for the new season. He was holding out for a little more money.

There was an exhibition game in Peterborough one night and Shack was told he would be playing

Buffalo Sabre Eddie Shack hitches a ride on California Seals' Gerry Ehman. (Robert B. Shaver)

79

for Rochester, a Leaf farm club — unless, of course, he came to terms. Shack said no way.

Later, in the hotel coffee shop, a brooding Shack sat down and ordered bacon and eggs. Rochester coach Joe Crozier, sitting nearby, called over to him.

"Eddie, if you're not going to play for us tonight, that means you're not on the team. And if you're not on the team, the Leaf organization doesn't pay for your food."

Shack didn't say a word, even when Crozier repeated himself. He chewed on his toast, stared at his coffee, and remained silent. For the third time Crozier reminded Shack that he would have to look after his own expenses, including the breakfast he was eating. Still there was no response. Shack sat there for five minutes pretending he was deaf. Only when he finished his meal and signed the team name to the bill did he regain his hearing.

Fergie Fought His Friends

WHEN JOHN FERGUSON TOILED for the Montreal Canadiens in the 1960s, he was hockey's toughest player. It took a brave man to challenge him. One who often did was pesky Bryan Watson of Detroit, even though he was one of Fergie's best friends. They had roomed together when both were rookies with the Canadiens, and a bond had been established. But it seemed to vanish when they met as rivals on the ice. Whenever Montreal played Detroit, it appeared as though they were trying to annihilate each other.

"That friendship stuff doesn't mean much to me

in a game," Watson told the late Paul Rimstead one day. "Why, I'd run my stick through Fergie just as fast as I would any other guy. Naw, I guess I wouldn't. Maybe just halfway through 'cause he's such a nice fellow."

"The guy [Watson] charged me into the boards one time, so I gave him a good punch on the head," Fergie said. "He spun around and gave me a two-hander with his stick. A good thing it missed my skull."

It is understandable that good pals, in the heat of battle, while playing for opposing teams, might come to blows. But Fergie very nearly flattened one of his own teammates during a game one night.

In New York the Canadiens were being manhandled by the New York Rangers. On the bench Fergie was seething. When the Rangers continued to beat up on the Habs, Fergie leaped up and was about to jump into the battle when a teammate restrained him.

"Aw, it's not worth it," he said.

Fergie won't name the player. But he does admit the fellow will never know how close he came to being the first NHLer to be punched out by one of his own teammates in the middle of a game.

PART

4

TALES AND TIDBITS FROM THE PAST

A Close Call for the Canadiens

FORMER MONTREAL CANADIEN Murray Wilson said to me at an old-timers' reception in Montreal not long ago, "I hear you're collecting hockey stories. Well, here's one all the reporters missed, and yet it came this close [he held up his thumb and index finger until they were almost touching] to being the most tragic hockey story of them all.

"It was without doubt the most frightening moment of my NHL career. The Canadiens were flying out of Detroit after a game one night in the late seventies. It was just another charter flight back home to Montreal. The plane was an old Fairchild F27. We took off and were right over London, Ontario, when suddenly we heard a thunderous noise — a big *kapow!* Smoke and fire could be seen shooting out of the left engine, and the whole compartment started filling up with smoke, as much smoke as you could imagine.

"The plane heeled over and started going down, dropping like a stone. It plunged from about 6,000 to 3,000 feet in a matter of seconds. It was like a scene from a movie where the plane spins wildly out of control and everyone panics. I looked around and every player's face was chalk-white. We were certain we were all about to die.

"Miraculously the pilot pulled the plane out of the dive a few hundred feet above the ground and slowly leveled it off. Only then could we breathe again. We made an emergency landing, limping into the airport at London, Ontario, on one engine.

"We couldn't get off that aircraft fast enough. The

85

club arranged for us to stay in a nearby hotel, and thank God the tavern was still open. That was probably the most profitable night the barkeeper ever had. After a couple of hours, the pilots came in and suggested that we get back on the plane. 'Everything's fixed,' they said. 'Come on, guys, let's go.'

"But some of us were still shaking. 'No bloody way!' we shouted. Steve Shutt, Yvan Cournoyer, and Guy Lafleur, along with the rest of us, flatly refused to get back on board. Coach Scotty Bowman wasn't about to argue with us that night. It's one debate he would have lost for sure. So the charter company had to arrange for a DC-9 to fly in the next morning, pick us up, and fly us home."

Zeidel Accuses Bruins of Anti-Semitism

IN 1967 LARRY ZEIDEL USED a standard business approach to find a job in the NHL. He sent each of the six new NHL expansion teams a brochure listing his many fine qualities, both as a player and as a candidate for a front-office position. Zeidel was 39 years old and had been plugging away as a rock-solid defenseman in many leagues for many years.

Few teams replied to Zeidel's brochure, but the Philadelphia Flyers, with two of their top rear guards (Joe Watson and Ed Van Impe) holding out, decided to take a chance. They signed Zeidel, and within a few days he was a regular on the Flyer blue line.

When a portion of the roof blew off the Spectrum in late February, the Flyers were forced to play some of their "home" games away from Philadelphia. One of these was in Toronto on March 7 versus the Boston Bruins. It was during this match that Zeidel became involved in a vicious stick-swinging duel with rambunctious Eddie Shack. Blood flowed and suspensions followed.

What shocked hockey fans were postgame statements from Zeidel, who maintained the battle was ignited because of anti-Semitic taunts hurled at him by players on the Boston bench. He insisted that one player said something about "not being satisfied until they put me in a gas chamber." Zeidel told Ed Conrad, a Philadelphia sportswriter: "Nearly the whole Boston team tried to intimidate me about being the only Jewish player in the NHL. They pulled this stuff when we played them earlier in the season. But when they brought up the business of the gas chamber and extermination, I didn't buy it." Zeidel, it was learned, had lost both his grandparents to the Nazi gas chambers during World War 11.

Zeidel mentioned Don Awrey, Tom Williams, and Gerry Cheevers as the mouthiest of the Bruins. Despite his ongoing feud with Shack, he didn't finger him as a racist.

Clarence Campbell and Flyer owner Ed Snider (a Jew himself) blamed the media for blowing the incident out of proportion. Perhaps one or both of these men had a friendly chat with Zeidel, because suddenly his lips were sealed when the subject was broached.

"I don't want to talk about it anymore," Zeidel told those who asked.

A Tragedy in Sudbury

THE MINING TOWN OF SUDBURY, ONTARIO, has been a hockey hotbed for as long as anyone who grew up in the area can remember. And once, on the night of January 26, 1899, when a huge crowd jammed the local arena, it became the scene of a hockey tragedy.

The game was between Sudbury and Mattawa, two fierce rivals, and the exciting contest had the fans on their feet. The gallery above the visiting team's goal was packed with spectators, many of them women.

Midway through the game, with Sudbury attacking the Mattawa goal, the crowd in the balcony surged forward in order to get a better view of the action below. Suddenly there was a loud crack as the wooden beam supporting the front of the gallery split in two. Power lines were snapped and the arena was plunged into darkness. People were thrown forward, and many tumbled over the railing and fell several feet onto the unsuspecting fans gathered below. About 30 spectators, their screams echoing throughout the arena, took the plunge. A few fell directly onto the ice and lay at the feet of the stunned hockey players. Some lay motionless, others writhed in pain, moaning and pleading for help.

Lights were called for and soon several lanterns appeared. Players on both teams and a number of volunteers gathered up the unconscious victims and brought them to the dressing rooms. Others were taken to a nearby drugstore.

Many of the the spectators who had been sitting

or standing below the gallery when it gave way suffered serious injuries. Their bodies had broken the falls of those in the gallery. Miraculously only one fatality was recorded. Several weeks after the incident a woman who had fallen from the gallery onto the ice died of her injuries.

He Wore Double Zero

WHEN BERNIE PARENT JOINED the Philadelphia Blazers of the World Hockey Association (he was originally signed by the Miami Screaming Eagles, a team that never materialized), he wore jersey number 00. If a curious member of the media asked him why he chose those numerals, he would reply, "Every time a puck gets past me and I look back in my net, I say 'Oh, oh.'"

Speaking of Strange Numerals

GOALIE ROYDON GUNN of the Saskatoon River Kings of the Central Hockey League wore .45 on his jersey during the 1993–94 season as a pun on his name and on the .45-caliber revolver. "It's such an oddity," said Craig Campbell of the Hockey Hall of Fame in Toronto, "that we'd like Gunn's jersey to add to our collection."

Meanwhile a hockey player in England decided to wear 102.1 on his back to help publicize the team sponsor, an FM radio station.

Teams They Never Played for Retired Their Jerseys

I HAVE OFTEN STUMPED fans and friends with the following trivia question: Name the players who had their numbers retired by NHL teams they never played for. The answer is: J. C. Tremblay and Johnny (Pie) McKenzie.

Let me explain how such an oddity happened. In 1972 J. C. Tremblay, a star defenseman for the Montreal Canadiens, jumped to the Quebec Nordiques of the WHA where he played for seven seasons. Just before the Nordiques joined the NHL for the 1979–80 season, Tremblay retired from hockey. A few months later the Nordiques (now in the NHL) retired his jersey number, even though he never played a game for the NHL version of the Nords.

All-Star defenseman J. C. Tremblay checks out the opposition.
(Robert B. Shaver)

A similar situation happened in Hartford, where Johnny McKenzie, during his WHA days with the New England Whalers, became a favorite with the team owner. Like J. C. Tremblay, Mackenzie retired from the game before the Whalers became a member of the NHL. But the NHL Whalers, even though he never wore one of their jerseys, held a special ceremony for McKenzie and retired his number 19.

Women Goalies Create History in Same Season

ON OCTOBER 30, 1993, a 22-year-old goalie from Glens Falls, New York, became the first woman in professional hockey history to be credited with a goaltending victory. Erin Whitten, playing for the Toledo Storm of the East Coast Hockey League, was the winning netminder when her team defeated the Dayton Bombers 6–5. The five-foot-five goalie began playing hockey at the age of eight and spent two years on the varsity team in high school. She went on to star for the New Hampshire Wildcats in women's college hockey before joining the Storm.

Whitten won her second pro game a couple of days later, and this time she may have set some kind of record, for she gave up 10 goals while her teammates were scoring 11. Nobody seemed to know if a goaltender had ever given up so many goals before and still been credited with a win. It is very unlikely.

Just one week after Whitten made her way into the history books, 21-year-old Manon Rheaume, a more-publicized woman goaltender playing in the same league, stopped 32 of 38 shots to help the Knoxville Cherokees to a 9–6 victory over the visiting Johnstown Chiefs. Knoxville fans booed when Rheaume wasn't announced as one of the three stars.

Then, early in 1994, goalie Kelly Dyer became the third woman to play a regular season game in professional hockey when she donned the pads for the West Palm Beach Blaze of the Sunshine League in Florida. The 27-year-old netminder played only 10 minutes against the Daytona Beach Sun Devils and stopped all seven shots she faced in a 6–2 win. The following day she played again, this time for 26 minutes, as the Blaze won 8–4. Dyer stopped 16 of 18 shots and shared the victory with regular netminder Scott Hopkins. Dyer was Tom Barrasso's backup goalie in high school hockey in Massachusetts and gained international recognition when she backstopped the U.S. women's team in two world championships.

Dick Rondeau's Most Memorable Game

MOST PROLIFIC GOAL SCORERS, when you ask them to name their most memorable game, have difficulty confining the choice to one contest. Not former U.S. college star Dick Rondeau, who was a top scorer for the Dartmouth College Indians many years ago. Dartmouth dominated college hockey during World War II, and in 1944 the Indians achieved their most one-sided victory, a 30–0 shellacking of Middlebury. Rondeau was unstoppable in this game, scoring 12 goals and adding 11 assists for 23 points — a once-in-a-lifetime performance. Incidentally, from 1942 to 1946, Dartmouth won 30 consecutive games, a U.S. college record that was snapped by Cornell (with Ken Dryden in goal) in 1969–70. Cornell set the new standard with 31 straight wins.

Suddenly a Merger — the NHL and the WHA

FOR TWO OR THREE YEARS in the seventies NHL moguls couldn't decide whether a merger with the rival World Hockey Association made sense or not. There were debates, arguments, and many meetings. President Clarence Campbell despised the WHA and prayed it would bankrupt itself out of existence. Toronto owner Harold Ballard, who had allowed some of his best players to slip away to the rival league because he wouldn't pay them enough to stay, told reporter Al Strachan, "I'm against it. If you run an appliance store and somebody steals all your washing machines, would you buy them back off him? That's what this merger thing boils down to."

Several NHL owners ignored Ballard and Campbell. Merger talks were held in Montreal, Chicago, Detroit, Toronto, and Key Largo, Florida. After the Chicago meeting, it was announced that a deal had been struck — the WHA would merge with the NHL. But the terms were so one-sided — the WHA teams would play in their own division, play mostly against one another, and wouldn't share in any TV revenues for some unspecified time — that the deal fell through.

At the Key Largo meetings in March 1979 the NHL governors decided there would be no more talk of merger. The idea was dead. Three weeks later there was a change of heart and the two leagues officially merged. The NHL welcomed four WHA franchises — Quebec, New England (later to become Hartford), Edmonton, and Calgary.

What prompted the sudden turnaround among the NHL owners? What catalyst moved them toward a merger? The answer is a simple one — beer sales.

Molson, the Canadian brewery, noticed that beer sales in western Canada were sagging. Why? Because the decision makers controlling the Montreal Canadiens had voted against the merger, depriving fans in Calgary and Edmonton of NHL hockey. Suddenly Molson's beverages tasted rather flat in the West. Some fans organized boycotts, and sales of Molson's products plummeted.

Suddenly the idea of a merger became a lot more appealing to the men who ran the Habs. Their no vote became a yes and the merger quickly became a reality.

Female Player Creates Unusual Attacking Style

WOMEN HAVE BEEN PLAYING HOCKEY for over 100 years, and one young lady became an instant star back in 1894. She scored three goals in a game between women's teams at McGill University, utilizing a technique that had never been seen before. This innovative player wore skates with an added accessory — a strap across each blade to prevent the puck from slipping through the opening.

Several times during the action she charged at the puck and trapped it between her skates. Then she used her stick, pushing it into the ice like a Venetian gondolier to keep her speed up. In this manner she propelled herself toward the opposing goal, and when she got close to her destination, she released the puck, swatting it with her stick at the rival goaltender. She scored three times this way.

Midway through her next foray up the ice, with the puck wedged firmly between her blades, a frustrated opponent came up with a simple, if unladylike, solution to the problem of gaining puck possession. She delivered a two-hander with her stick to the puck carrier's feet — with predictable results. The scorer of the hat trick howled in pain and collapsed to the ice, releasing the puck. The stick-wielding woman was banished from the game and suspended for the rest of the season.

Bend Over, Mabel, Here They Come Again

ANOTHER PLOY FEMALE PLAYERS used successfully time after time early in the century wasn't possible in men's games. When the opposing team moved in on goal, several defenders would form a group in front of their netminder and bend over. Crouching allowed their long skirts to fan out along the ice, leaving few openings for an opponent to take a shot on goal or pass the puck to a teammate.

Winnipeg Fans Wildly Excited About Cup Series in 1902

THE WINNIPEG VICS CAPTURED the Stanley Cup in 1902, defeating the Toronto Wellingtons. It was after one of these games that newsmen accused the visitors of smoking on the bench while the game was in progress. The Wellingtons had a complaint of their own. The penalties, under western rules, were often far too long. The penalized player had to serve a "game," which was a common word for the time leading up to a goal. In other words, he couldn't return to the ice until a goal was scored. It was finally agreed that the penalty time for a minor infraction would be two minutes.

For the second Cup series against Montreal the teams couldn't agree on a referee. Two men qualified, McFarlane and Quinn. Finally there was a coin toss and McFarlane won. But that gentleman refused the assignment initially. Why? Because Montreal had favored Quinn, which hurt McFarlane's feelings.

Prior to the series the temperature in Winnipeg soared, reaching 62 degrees Fahrenheit. The ice began to melt in the Winnipeg arena and workers mopped the surface with blankets. Even though much of the water was absorbed, the games were played in slush.

According to the *Winnipeg Telegram,* young men "climbed, squeezed, burrowed their way in — free. One fan would pay and once inside he would open a window 30 feet above the ground. His friends used ladders 'borrowed' from the nearby Hudson's Bay Company and snuck in the window. A whole squad of policemen missed the illegal entry. They were too busy watching the game and thinking of the four dollars they were to receive for keeping an eye out for gatecrashers."

Interest in the series was equally high back in Montreal. Over 500 fans jammed the Montreal Amateur Athletic Association gymnasium to get wireless reports, while in the streets of the city an estimated 10,000 watched and waited for the newspapers to put out bulletin boards with updates on the action.

Winnipeg won the first match, played in pools of water, by a 1–0 score. Montreal bounced back with a 5–0 shutout in game two. Big Billy Nicholson, Montreal's 300-pound goalie, handled all shots thrown his way in a masterly fashion.

It was in game three that the visitors earned a nickname that would stay with them forever. The bigger Winnipeg players crashed through time after time, but the Montrealers didn't flinch and hung on tenaciously, protecting a 2–1 lead, which became the winning score. A telegrapher at rinkside flashed the news to Montreal. "The visitors are taking terrible punishment but they are hanging on like little men of iron." From that day on the Montrealers were known as "the little men of iron."

The goaltending of big Billy Nicholson was the difference in the series. He allowed just two goals in the three games.

As a final note, Nicholson's daughter, Helen Nicholson Wolthro, from Cornwall, Ontario, visited my hockey museum at Colborne, Ontario, recently and was surprised to find a photo of her late father on display. Later I visited Mrs. Wolthro at her home in Cornwall, and she placed (on loan) the goal stick used by her father in the 1902 Stanley Cup series. Mrs. Wolthro (née Nicholson), in the 1930s at age 15, was a star player on a Montreal women's team, the leading scorer in her league. She played before as many as 6,000 spectators in one championship series.

Pittsburgh Is Mad About Hockey

SUCH A HEADLINE would be perfectly understandable in the 1990s, especially after the Penguins' back-to-back Stanley Cup wins in 1991 and 1992. But the above headline is culled from the sports page of a Pittsburgh paper — not in the 1990s after consecutive Stanley Cup wins — but from a Pittsburgh sports page printed over 90 years ago — in 1902.

Two major reasons for the popularity of hockey in Pittsburgh at the turn of the century were artificial ice and a posh new arena. Artificial ice allowed for a full season of play without fear of games being canceled or postponed because of warm weather. And Canadian teams, eager to play on the much-talked-about surface, were quick to accept invitations to play in the Steel City. Many star players from Canada were lured to Pittsburgh with job offers and other enticements, so the competition was always keen.

The manager of a Kingston, Ontario, team returned from a series of games in Pittsburgh in 1902 and gave the following report to the Toronto *Globe:*

Pittsburgh is hockey crazy. Over 10,000 people turned out for our three games there. The general admission being 35 cents and 75 cents for a box seat. The receipts were about $4,000, but all that we got for our share was $350, which, after expenses, will leave about enough to buy some postage stamps.

But the Pittsburgh rink is a dream. If there was anything like it in Toronto the people would turn out in thousands instead of hundreds to see a game. Around the ice surface, which is about 275 feet long by 125 feet wide [the standard NHL surface is 200 feet by 85 feet], the seats are arranged in tiers above the boxes which are fitted up luxuriously. The surroundings are more suited to a theatre than for a rink. Every move by the players can be seen distinctly by the spectators, the place being lighted by thousands of incandescent and other lamps. No expense has been spared and the uniformed attendants are to be seen everywhere. The band is always in attendance and there is every convenience for patrons, who, for the skating sessions, can get their blades sharpened or acquire a pair of skates without going outside the building. What a marvellous place it is.

The manager had only one complaint about the trip to Pittsburgh and that was about a hometown goal judge. He told the *Globe:*

We played the Bankers team there and they beat us 3–2. But one of their goals was scored after the referee's whistle had blown. Our boys let up when they heard the whistle and one of the Bankers put the puck in the net. The goal judge raised his arm, ruled it a goal and the referee agreed with him. Later, we scored a goal and at first the same goal judge allowed it, then he disallowed it. He told me afterwards that the puck had indeed gone inside the posts, but it was batted out so quickly that he thought he might have been mistaken and in order to avoid any trouble he did not put up his hand. Have you ever heard of such a thing?

Those Crybabies

ON FEBRUARY 28, 1902, team executives of the the Montreal Victorias held a meeting after which they lodged a protest with the league over the result of a game played two days earlier. The Vics maintained that the puck used in the match wasn't a regulation one. It was slightly smaller than the regulation disk. Furthermore, it wasn't a new puck. Therefore, they maintained, the score shouldn't count and their defeat should be erased from the records.

The Vics' protest was not only thrown out but the team was ridiculed and universally accused of being a "bunch of poor sports and crybabies." One Toronto sports editor wrote: "The Montreal Vics must expect their protest to be considered by a committee from some institution for the feeble-minded if they have any idea it will prevail." Another editor wrote: "They're grown up but still babies. They claim that the puck was not regulation size but they agreed to play with it. Only when they lost did they decide to protest."

The First Play-by-Play Announcer

IN MY PREVIOUS VOLUME, *More It Happened in Hockey,* I dispel the myth that Foster Hewitt was the world's first play-by-play hockey announcer. Credit is given to Pete Parker of Regina, who preceded Hewitt into a rinkside booth by several days. On March 14, 1923, Parker handled the first complete broadcast of a professional game heard on radio station CKCK in Regina. Eight days later, on March 22, 1923, Hewitt called the play of a senior amateur game from the Mutual Street Arena in Toronto over the *Toronto Star*'s radio station CFCA.

Parker was obviously miffed that Hewitt always maintained that he was the first. In a letter to me dated March 4, 1972, Parker stated: "On at least two TV panel shows on which he has appeared, Hewitt has calmly stated that his game on March 22, 1923, was the first ever to be broadcast via radio. In Foster's book, *Hockey Night in Canada,* published in 1953, Foster moves the date back a year, declaring, 'In 1921 I broadcast my first hockey game . . .' This is a ridiculous statement for the simple reason that the *Toronto Star*'s radio station, CFCA, didn't start operating until late in 1922."

Parker was quick to add a third name to the mix, that of Norman Albert of Toronto. In his view Albert may warrant the title "World's First Hockey Announcer." According to *Toronto Star* files, Albert broadcast a portion of a game between Midland and North Toronto from the Mutual Street Arena — six weeks before Parker made his debut and seven weeks prior to Hewitt's first broadcast. In a second letter to me in 1972, Parker writes: "I sent a letter to Norman Albert in Toronto and a few days later I received a reply from his wife. She said her husband was too ill to write. She mentioned that Norman had often told her he had broadcast a hockey game before Foster Hewitt but had never done anything about it. Norman worked in the editorial department at the *Toronto Star* at the same time as Foster and was 'drafted' to do the game on February 8, 1923. Unfortunately, Foster has chosen to let the public continue to think that the achievement belongs to him, instead of to Norman Albert. Apparently his conscience never bothered him."

Others may argue that Foster Hewitt wasn't the first play-by-play announcer, but who can deny that he became the most famous? Almost single-handedly he made Saturday night hockey an institution across Canada.

Hockey "Firsts" Were Numerous in the WHA

WHEN THE WHA SPRANG UP in the 1970s, the new league soon became renowned for some bizarre hockey "firsts." Many of them occurred during the initial season of the WHA's existence. For example:

- The WHA introduced the postgame shoot-out to cut down on the number of ties. In its first test the shoot-out enabled the Houston Aeros to edge the Minnesota Fighting Saints 7–6. The score at the end of regulation time was 4–4. It remained 4–4 after a 10-minute overtime period. After that it required 18 free shots (each team scored twice) before journeyman Don Grierson emerged as the hero, scoring on shot number 17. Minnesota's Terry Ball missed on the next shot and the Aeros won the game. The shoot-out experiment was later abandoned.

- The Los Angeles Sharks opened their first season at home on Friday the 13th against Houston. The pucks hadn't been frozen prior to the game and bounced around like rubber balls. And when the Zamboni driver flooded the ice at the intermission, black liquid oozed out from under the machine and covered a large patch of ice.

- The Philadelphia Blazers called a news conference to announce the signing of Fred Creighton as coach. But Creighton changed his mind at the last minute and didn't show up. The team then announced the signing of Murray Williamson as general manager, but he quit on the day the announcement was made. Williamson's successor, Dave Creighton, showed only slightly more dedication to the position. He stayed around until the team went 1–8 before he resigned. By then player-coach John Mackenzie had also thrown in the towel. He was replaced by Phil Watson.

- Players on the Los Angeles Sharks scrambled to score the first hat trick in club history. They had heard that a handsome reward awaited the man who achieved the first three-goal game. When Gary

Veneruzzo accomplished the feat, the club owner gave him two tickets for a trip to Hawaii.

- Danny Lawson, who scored a mere 10 goals with the NHL's Buffalo Sabres in the previous season, became the fledgling league's first 50-goal scorer. The Blazers' Lawson scored number 50 against Ottawa on February 22.
- Goalie Bernie Parent dropped a bombshell on the Philadelphia Blazers during a playoff series with Cleveland. Parent, on a five-year $750,000 contract, claimed the Blazers had failed to deposit the final $100,000 insurance on his salary. So he walked out on the team and refused to play. Without Parent the Blazers were no match for the Cleveland Crusaders and were eliminated in four straight games.

Initiations Are on the Wane

THE BARBARIC RITUAL OF INITIATING a rookie player into pro hockey has been around forever. The shaving of heads and pubic hair and other rites of passage based on degradation and humiliation are slowly being phased out of hockey. And about time, too.

The anti-initiation groups began to surface in 1988 after a bizarre hazing of freshmen hockey players at Kent State University in Ohio led to several arrests. Five rookies — their heads covered with sacks — were taken to a basement and stripped. They were placed on benches, their hands were bound with tape, and their heads and genitals were shaved. A hot ointment was liberally applied to the genitals of some, ice and snow placed in the same general area of the others. Following the shaving, the freshmen were forced to drink a mixture of beer and rum, using a funnel, and one player became so ill that he was hospitalized for three days. Police arrived and charged five players with hazing, which is against the law in Ohio. The freshmen were charged with underage consumption of alcohol.

In Ontario, during the same season, an 18-year-old player was charged with assault after rookies on a Junior B team were forced to masturbate in front of older players.

Recently player agents have begun writing anti-hazing clauses into their clients' contracts with the team agreeing to pay substantial financial penalties if hazing occurs. Agent Rick Curran said, "I had one client who was so afraid of being shaved that he was physically ill for a few days." Don Meehan, another agent, added, "I know of a case where a kid had his head shoved into a toilet to make him sick. It's childish, humiliating, and there's no good reason for it."

In recent years several NHL teams have abolished hazing and replaced the ritual with the costly custom of having the rookies pay for a team dinner. When Alexander Daigle picked up the tab after the Ottawa Senators feasted, he wound up $5,000 lighter in the wallet.

They Battled for Tickets

FRIGID TEMPERATURES FAILED to cool off Ottawa fans on the eve of a big game with the Montreal Wanderers in February 1907.

More than 1,000 fans waited in line for hours in subzero weather to buy tickets for the game. Many in the crowd waited all night. By morning the mob was such that windows were broken, hats and coats torn and destroyed, and police had to use their batons frequently to quell the impatient gathering. Ottawa's Elgin Street was packed with people. Plate-glass windows in the offices nearby were smashed as fans fought to retain their place in line, and additional policemen had to fight their way through the throng to prevent further damage. It was finally announced that the sale of tickets wouldn't take place until later in the day at Dey's Arena. The fans rushed to form a new line at the arena, only to discover that a mere handful of tickets were on sale. When ticket sales were cut off, the mob outside, half frozen and furious, launched large chunks of ice at the building, breaking most of the windows.

Oxford Versus Cambridge — a Fierce Hockey Rivalry

ENGLAND'S TWO OLDEST HOCKEY TEAMS represent the nation's two oldest universities, Oxford and Cambridge, and the on-ice competition between the prestigious institutions has been going on for more than 100 years.

In 1885 Oxford and Cambridge journeyed to St. Moritz, Switzerland, to engage in the first game of hockey ever played on the continent. With newspapers strapped to their shins and blades strapped to their boots, the dark blues of Oxford shut out the light blues of Cambridge 6–0. After that encounter, the clubs called a time-out that lasted 15 years before agreeing to a second match, this one at the Prince Stanley Skating Club in London in 1900. Oxford won again 7–6.

The 1900 game was played with bandy sticks and a lacrosse ball instead of a puck. Several years later, in 1909, at Wengen, Switzerland, the teams batted a wooden block around, presumably because someone forgot to pack the lacrosse ball. One of the players on the Oxford team of this era was Lester B. Pearson, future prime minister of Canada.

When the 1948 Cambridge team ventured onto the ice for the big game at Dunfermline, they discovered the arena roof was supported by a huge pole situated at center ice. Oxford had practiced many times in the rink, and the Oxford players were accustomed to avoiding the pole. They were also adept at luring the Cambridge boys in the direction of the pole, and more than one crashed into it. Oxford won 5–2. As one reporter observed, "It was almost as if Oxford had an extra man on the ice — the pole."

Future prime minister Lester B. Pearson (front right) waits for a pass from an Oxford University teammate in a match with a Swiss club, circa 1922–23. (National Archives of Canada)

The 1955 match was slightly one-sided. The Cambridge netminder faced an even 100 shots, turning aside 71, while the Oxford goal guardian was required to stop only two. Oxford won 29–0.

They Walked Out on Team Canada '72

WHEN THEY QUIT AND CAME HOME, they were castigated and reviled. They were called quitters, traitors, defectors. They were the Infamous Four. Their sin was to leave Moscow before game five of the emotionally charged Summit Series of 1972, and their names were Vic Hadfield, Jocelyn Guevremont, Richard Martin, and Gilbert Perreault. Hadfield bore the brunt of the abuse. As a veteran NHL player, he was expected to know better. The other three were rookies in the league. It was assumed they were too young to realize what they were doing.

None of the four had seen much action in what has accurately been portrayed as the most exciting series ever played, one that brought a nation to a standstill during each of the final four games in Moscow. Hadfield, a 50-goal shooter in the previous season, was the first player to express his discontent. When he failed to see his name in the Team Canada lineup prior to game five, he told coach Harry Sinden he wanted to go home. Sinden consulted Alan Eagleson, who arranged for Hadfield to depart on the next flight to Canada. Guevremont (Vancouver Canucks), Perreault, and Martin (both of the Buffalo Sabres) were quick to follow. Veteran sports columnist Jim Coleman later pointed out:

"The young men who went home lost the opportunity to share what might have been the most glorious winning experience of their lives."

True. But when they decided to leave, they felt like so much excess baggage, unemployed and useless. It hurt. It was an attitude that differed sharply from that of goalie Ed Johnston, who never missed a meeting or a practice — and didn't get to play a single minute of a single game! No one could have ached more for a chance to play than Johnston.

Richard Martin said: "The team had plenty of players, and when we asked the coaches if there was any chance we'd play, any chance at all, they basically said no. I really felt I owed it to my employers, the Buffalo Sabres, to come home and get ready for the NHL season. All four of us felt the same way. We left the team on good terms, at least we thought we did. Then we came home to be called traitors and everything else. It came as a shock."

More than 20 years have passed since the players climbed aboard that plane and left their mates in Moscow. Now we wonder what all the fuss was about. Why was so much criticism heaped on the Infamous Four? Should they forever be branded as deserters?

At a reunion of Team Canada '72 in 1985, team leader Phil Esposito said: "It's really terrible what those four guys have had to put up with over the years. They did what they felt was right at the time. Who knows how many of us wouldn't have done the same thing if we'd been in their position? They shouldn't have to carry that kind of a load around. It's just not fair."

Martin had a final comment on the decision to come home: "I've often thought about what I would do now if I was placed in the same situation. I can honestly say I wouldn't change anything. If I had to do it all over again, I'd do exactly the same thing."

The First Expansion Team to Win the Cup

HOCKEY BROADCASTERS FORTUNATE enough to be in the booth when a Stanley Cup final series is decided never forget the moment. One that shines in my memory is the 1974 championship won by the Philadelphia Flyers, the first so-called expansion team to capture the Cup.

I was with NBC then, working with Tim Ryan and Ted Lindsay, and our playoff coverage was seen throughout North America. The Flyers had two major obstacles to overcome before capturing the Cup. The first was the New York Rangers, with a lineup boasting talented old pros like Ed Giacomin, Brad Park, Rod Gilbert, Jean Ratelle, and Vic Hadfield. The series produced seven tension-packed, bruising games, and in game four in New York, Flyer defenseman Barry Ashbee's career came to a sudden end when he was struck in the eye by a Dale Rolfe shot. When Ashbee went down, I was holding a wireless microphone at rinkside. As the gate in front of me opened, I impulsively followed the medical people onto the ice and got a report on the injury from linesman Matt Pavelich. It was a television "first," and later it brought a reprimand from NHL president Clarence Campbell: "Mr. McFarlane, don't go on the ice!"

After ousting New York, the Flyers faced the even

more formidable Boston Bruins. There was Orr, Esposito, Hodge, Cashman, Bucyk — one of the highest scoring machines ever assembled. Boston won the opener on home ice 3–2 with Orr the hero, scoring the winning goal in the final half minute of play. The second game has often been called the most decisive in Flyer history. Moose Dupont tied the score with 52 seconds on the clock, and Bobby Clarke popped in the winner after 12:01 of overtime. Clarke leaped into the air like a high jumper when the red light flashed.

The Flyers won two more at the Spectrum, then lost in Boston 5–1. For game six there was a surprise. Kate Smith, the Flyers' good-luck charm, made a personal appearance at the Spectrum, and when she sang "God Bless America" before the opening whistle, the roof almost came off. While Bernie Parent performed like a wizard in the Flyers' goal, Rick MacLeish slammed in the only goal of the game and the Flyers were champions at last. I remember the incredible ovation, the fans leaping and skidding over the ice, the bedlam in the dressing room where I did postgame interviews. Off to one side, wearing dark glasses, stood Barry Ashbee, tears of happiness running down his cheeks. Three years later Ashbee, at age 37 and groomed to be the next Flyers' coach, would die of leukemia.

The following day there was a hastily organized mammoth parade to celebrate the Flyers' victory and the turnout was incredible. It was the largest victory parade in Stanley Cup history. An estimated two million Philadelphians honored their beloved team with an unprecedented outpouring of affection and gratitude.

Observations on Ladies at Play

WOMEN HAVE BEEN PLAYING hockey for more than 100 years, and some of the reports and observations on early games make fascinating reading. For example, in 1896 an Ottawa correspondent wrote: "That the Alpha and Rideau Ladies hockey teams can play hockey was well demonstrated at the Rideau rink last night. Both teams played grandly and surprised hundreds of the sterner sex who went to the match expecting to see many ludicrous scenes and have many good laughs. Indeed, before they were there very long, the men's sympathies and admiration went out to the players and they became wildly enthusiastic."

After another game, one that involved Lady Minto, the wife of the governor general, it was reported that "The ladies on both sides played with a vim quite foreign to their natures. Lady Minto played at cover point and the manner in which she went up the ice was a revelation. Mr. George Meagher, the champion figure skater of the world, said: 'I have seen all the best skaters in the world and I consider the Countess of Minto to be the peer of them all. Lady Minto has all the qualifications of the finished expert on skates, which are grace, suppleness and strength.'"

After a game in Belleville in 1902 between the hometown Scorchers and the visiting Kingston Aerials, it was commented that "The Kingston maidens were good skaters and stickhandlers but when their age and weight are taken into account, it is no wonder they won the game 5–0. The Kingston team were composed of women, some of them old enough to be the mothers of the Belleville girls, but then they cannot help getting old."

In 1905 there was this account of a troublemaker: "Miss Allen was ruled off for a minute for being a bad girl. She checked one of the Broadview girls real hard." And in 1907, when a Toronto team hosted the girls from Waterloo, Ontario, it was reported that:

> Wads of gum were handled gracefully by the Toronto ladies, and it evidently helped some at the close. Combs were strewn about the ice in greater or less profusion, but the players never took on the run-down look that appears in the "before" and "after" circulars. They were always trim and neat — even when tired.
>
> One of the Wellington ladies, her hair full of hairpins, utilized the intermission time to indulge in a considerable amount of hairdressing before she consented to return to the ice.
>
> Referee Bruce Ridpath was ungallant enough to send five players to the penalty bench. His sentence was a minute each time but the timekeeper, Bert Shortt, was so susceptible to the charms of those penalized that he shortened the minute each time most outrageously.
>
> Miss Hamilton accidentally smote a spectator with her stick and paused to beg his forgiveness.
>
> The Waterloo girls gave the Wellingtons the busiest five minutes you ever saw. If there hadn't been so many long skirts in the way, Waterloo must have scored. But "them Wellintuns" just gathered around like a sewing circle listening to a bit of scandal, bent their knees until their skirts touched

the ice, and — well, only a pair of shears or a 10.2 inch gun would have cleared the way to the net.

Boston's 45-year Jinx

IN 1943 THE BOSTON BRUINS lost a playoff hockey series to the Montreal Canadiens. From that wartime year to the spring of 1988 the Bruins met the Habs 18 times in postseason play — and lost every time. In 1988 the long string of losses came to an end when the Bruins pushed Montreal aside four games to one in a division semifinal series.

The All-time Worst Team

PITY THE NHL TEAMS that can't seem to get things right. In 80 years of NHL play some woeful squads have humiliated themselves over the course of a season or seasons.

Which was the all-time worst? Was it the Philadelphia Quakers or the Quebec Bulldogs, both of whom won but four of their 24 league games in 1930–31? Quebec wouldn't have won even four times if it hadn't been for superstar Joe Malone, who scored 39 goals, more than the rest of his teammates combined. Was it the moribund Pittsburgh Pirates of 1929–30, who stumbled to five victories in 44 games and then were chased out of town? Was it the 1992–93 San Jose Sharks or Ottawa Senators who managed some modern-day futility records — the Sharks losing 32 of their home games, the Senators dropping 40 on the road? No,

San Jose, Ottawa, and the other clubs mentioned above escape the ignomy of being branded the worst team ever.

Using winning percentage as a measuring rod, the stamp of failure and shame is affixed to the woeful Washington Capitals of 1974–75. The Caps compiled a record of 8–67–5 for 21 points and a winning percentage of .131. The Caps gave up 446 goals during the season — their first in the NHL — 100 more than the Minnesota North Stars, the next most porous team, who surrendered 341.

Incredibly the Caps finished 92 points behind three division champions, Montreal, Buffalo, and Philadelphia. All three compiled 113 points.

Hockey More Violent at Turn of Century

THE QUESTION OFTEN COMES UP: Was hockey more violent in the good old days? Picking a month and a season at random, I came up with January 1907 and perused the sports pages for episodes of hockey violence that month — and there were plenty. For example:

- January 2: Referee Magnus Flett has advised the Manitoba Hockey League to expel Dey of Portage la Prairie for his foul play in the game with Brandon. He put Leader and Armstrong out of the game by using his stick on their heads.
- January 4: It is claimed that McIvor of the Goderich club, on New Year's Eve, when neither he nor his check was playing the

puck, skated down on Cole (a deaf mute on the Clinton team), striking him from behind with his stick, knocking him down, and fracturing his jaw in three places. The referee at once ruled McIvor off for 10 minutes. McIvor was later arrested, charged with assault, and suspended for the rest of the season.

- January 7: In the Calumet–Soo game on Saturday night there was a sensational incident when goaltender Jones of the Soo laid out Bert Morrison by hitting him over the head. In the Houghton–Pittsburgh game Campbell of Pittsburgh assaulted referee Melville and was given the extreme International League penalty — three minutes.

- January 9: The *Soo Express* says: "Marty Walsh, one of the cleverest men in hockey, had to be removed to the hospital, suffering from a compound fracture of the ankle. The attack upon Walsh was brutal, two of the heaviest men of the Calumet team jumping onto the boy, and it is said that he was choked and slugged while prone on the ice. Little Walsh was unconscious and suffered intense pain."

- January 9: The first game in the Saskatchewan League was very rough. A Regina spectator fell out of the gallery onto the ice and was unconscious for some time. Later a Regina spectator jumped over the fence and struck Coldwell, the Moose Jaw umpire. A free-for-all ensued, ending in several spectators going to jail.

- January 13: This report followed a donnybrook between Ottawa and the Wanderers in Montreal. "In the match, Baldy Spittal was said to have tried to split Blatchford's head open by bringing down his hockey stick on it with all the force he could muster. Blatchford was carried off with his blood spilling on the ice. Alf Smith was reported to have skated up to Hod Stuart and, hitting him across the temple with his stick, laid him out like a corpse. Meanwhile, Harry Smith was cracking Ernie Johnston across the face with his stick, breaking his nose and spilling more blood." Follow-up coverage in the papers expressed the writers' outrage: "They should get six months in jail is the opinion as to the game's brutalities. And old players say it was the worst exhibition of butchery they ever saw."
- January 16: From a report on the game between Newmarket and Toronto St. Georges: "Doyle and Kennedy 'rough housed' at every opportunity. Doyle on one occasion let fly his stick at an opponent who was skating away from him. Kennedy bumped into everybody and twice threw his stick at a St. Georges player when a score appeared to be imminent."
- January 27: There was a follow-up story to the January 12 donnybrook between Montreal and Ottawa: "The three Ottawa players, Spittal, Alf Smith and Harry Smith, for whom warrants were recently issued for assault on Wanderer players, appeared in

the police court on Saturday and were admitted to bail, to appear on Wednesday next for a hearing." On the following Wednesday Alf Smith and Baldy Spittal were fined $20 apiece and were bound over to keep the peace for 12 months. Nose breaker Harry Smith was found not guilty.

- January 29: A report read: "F. C. Chittick, referee of the final Wanderers–Kenora match in Montreal, will in all probability take legal action against Tom Hodge of Montreal, an ex-member of the Wanderers Executive, for an assault which Mr. Chittick says was committed after the match. It is said that the referee was walking to one of the dressing rooms when Mr. Hodge struck him from behind, being angered at Mr. Chittick's handling of the game, in which Wanderers were defeated, with the consequent loss of the Stanley Cup. Hodge will be remembered as referee at Ottawa when the Toronto Marlboros went there after the Stanley Cup. He saw nothing wrong so far as Ottawa's tactics were concerned, and they whaled, slashed, cross-checked and fouled the Marlboros to their heart's content."

Was hockey as violent then as it is today? Indeed it was — even more so. If we had chronicled episodes of hockey violence for another six weeks — into March 1907 — we would have come across a fatality on ice. A Cornwall star, Owen McCourt, was killed in a game against the Ottawa Vics. Struck over the head by an opponent's stick, McCourt was

118

Fights have always been a part of hockey, as this dust-up between the Maple Leafs and the Blackhawks back in the days of the old six-team league can attest. (Hockey Hall of Fame)

rushed to hospital where he died. Charlie Masson of Ottawa was charged with manslaughter and put on trial. He was acquitted on April 10 when teammates testified it was another player's stick that had struck McCourt that night.

PART

5

CURIOUS
CAPERS

Hockey's Number One Sex Symbol

WHEN RON DUGUAY, a good-looking kid from Sudbury, joined the New York Rangers in 1977, his teammates initiated him by shaving his head. Poor Doogie. His hair meant everything to him. It had been long and curly, and when he skated down the ice at full speed, it flowed behind him, attracting the eye of every woman in the rink.

Until his hair grew back he was just another hockey player. With a new growth on top he quickly became the most popular of all the Rangers, at least with female fans. He was hockey's number one sex symbol, and in a very short time he received more attention in the New York papers for his off-ice activites than any Ranger in history.

He was linked romantically with Cher, Margaret Trudeau, Bianca Jagger, Patti Lupone, and Cheryl Tiegs. Major league company. Private limos whisked him from club to club where beautiful women flocked to his side. He talked about his love life candidly to a reporter from a well-known sex magazine and was photographed on the cover surrounded by several topless models. In the article he said he preferred older women because "they don't just lie around and drool over me. Besides, they're hotter lovers." When asked if he preferred making love or scoring on a breakaway, he answered, "Scoring on a breakaway because I haven't scored on too many breakaways." Another magazine, *Harper's Bazaar,* named him as one of America's ten most wanted men — wanted by women, that is. Again he was photographed with a bevy of beauties touching his body. He landed a modeling contract for a major jeans manufacturer,

Sex symbol Ron Duguay, flowing locks free of helmet, sails down the ice.

and women who watched his commercials on TV talked about his fabulous derriere.

In time it all ended, of course. He got older, he was traded, first to Detroit, then to Pittsburgh, back to New York for a few games, and then on to Los Angeles, racking up 12 seasons in the NHL, 274 goals, 346 assists, and 620 points. Along the way he married and settled down. But those years in New York were fun while they lasted. Arduous, too. It isn't easy living up to a reputation as hockey's number one sex symbol.

The Bear Wrestler

WHEN JOE LOUIS first retired as the heavyweight champion of the world in 1949, he left without much money. So he took a job with the Barnum and Bailey Circus to make ends meet. His job was to referee wrestling matches between a mean-looking circus bear and anyone brave or foolish enough to try to put the furry creature down.

Sometimes it was difficult to persuade local strongmen to climb into the ring with an animal that looked so ferocious. But not in Joliette, Quebec, where a 16-year-old hockey player named Marcel Bonin leaped fearlessly over the ropes.

"Mr. Louis, I'll wrestle this bear. Let's see how tough he really is," Bonin said.

The ensuing struggle is still talked about by old-timers in Joliette. Young Bonin, they say, fought the muzzled monster to a draw. *Mais oui,* he failed to put the mangy bruin down, but the citizens of Joliette cheered young Bonin, anyway, when the match was over.

Only recently, when I chatted with Bonin at the Montreal Forum, did he confess there was a reason for his bravado that day. "Sure, the bear had a muzzle and he'd been declawed, but still, he was a very big, tough old bear. Must have weighed 400 pounds. But Marcel Bonin is not crazy. I went to see that bear in the morning, before the match, and I fed him and played with him until we were pretty good friends. He was glad to see me when I jumped into the ring.

"I wrestled that same bear many times in the small towns in Quebec. Nobody else wanted to take a chance with him. I think we put on a pretty good show for the people.

"My friend Marcel Pronovost was playing with Detroit in those days, and when I came up to play hockey with the Red Wings, he told everybody I was a tough little bear wrestler from Joliette. The papers made a big thing of that."

Bonin was later traded to the Montreal Canadiens where he played on four Stanley Cup-winning teams. One year, hoping to change his scoring luck, he borrowed a pair of Rocket Richard's old gloves. "Maybe they'll help me get out of my slump," he told Richard. In the next eight games Bonin scored eight goals.

Death of a Fan

OVER THE YEARS thousands of pucks have been sent flying in among the spectators at hockey games. Occasionally unwary fans are bruised or bloodied by the hard rubber disks, but seldom do these injuries prove fatal.

One of the earliest known deaths resulting from such an incident took place in Beamsville, Ontario, in the spring of 1902. A teenage boy, Gordon Groves, was a spectator at a game when a puck flew over the boards and struck him on the head. He appeared dazed but didn't lose consciousness. Young Groves was even able to retrieve the puck and keep it as a souvenir. The next day he assured his parents he was able to attend school but, once there, he complained of a severe headache and feeling sick. His condition worsened and in a few minutes he was dead. His death was attributed to the blow he had received at the hockey game.

One Way to Beat the Russians

PAUL PROVOST, an Ottawa boy who played hockey in the forties and fifties, was too small for a pro career. So he opted for a career in European hockey where, at five foot seven and 125 pounds, he became a big man in the scoring summaries.

One year he signed on as player-coach of the Chamonix team in France and was impressed with the lengths his players would go to avoid a loss. Provost's team was involved in a close game with a touring Russian club one night. The contest was held at an outdoor ice rink during a blinding snowstorm. Late in the game the Chamonix club was trailing by a goal, and Provost urged his men to find a way to get the equalizer. Moments later one of them did. The goal judge signaled a goal and the score was tied.

Only later did Provost find out how the puck went in. "I was skating around in the snow," one of his players confessed, "and couldn't see three feet in front of me when the puck struck my foot. It bounced up, so I caught it and hid it in my glove. Then I skated in behind the Russian goalie and dropped it in the net. The referee saw it lying there and so did the goal judge. They decided to call it a goal. I guess I was the only one out there who knew what really happened. And I'm not telling anyone but you, Coach."

Why Stemmer Got Traded

PETE STEMKOWSKI WAS a key member of the last Toronto Maple Leaf team to win the Stanley Cup — the Leafs of 1967. He was a popular Leaf and a happy Leaf. He was even naive enough to figure he would be with the Toronto organization forever.

That was why it came as such a shock when he

was traded to Detroit a year after celebrating the Leafs' Stanley Cup victory. But he put past triumphs behind him and concentrated on having some big seasons with his new club. His first season in a Red Wing uniform was excellent — he doubled the number of goals he had scored as a Leaf in 1967. And the next year was even better — a 25-goal season, an impressive total for the sixties. Why then was he suddenly sent packing from the Red Wings in 1969?

Well, it seems his off-ice sense of humor wasn't appreciated by Ned Harkness, who was the team's coach and general manager back then. Harkness had been a highly successful coach in U.S. college hockey at Cornell, but he had never been with a pro team in his life.

The first time he met Stemkowski he told him to get a haircut. Stemmer made a date with the barber, but not enough hair was clipped to please the coach. Stemkowski got a second haircut and mailed the hair clippings to Harkness to prove he was following orders.

Then came the fateful day when Stemkowski entered the Red Wing dressing room wearing the coach's beloved Cornell windbreaker and baseball cap. The jacket and cap had become a Ned Harkness trademark in college. Stemmer blew a whistle and began to put on a show for his grinning teammates.

"Gimme a C!" he shouted. "Gimme an O, gimme an R, gimme an N!"

But before he could finish spelling out Cornell in his best cheerleader fashion, the door popped open and in walked Harkness. Stemkowski never got to finish his routine. His performance was cut short and so was his stint in Detroit. A few days later he was traded to New York for Larry Brown.

Thirty Minutes for Talking

HALL OF FAMER Frank Frederickson, who once scored 41 goals in 30 games for the Victoria club of the old Pacific Coast Hockey league, was as fine a player as ever laced up skates. His only problem was his penchant for talking. He voiced opinions on everything, to the dismay of his family and friends and, of course, to every player, penalty timekeeper, and referee in organized hockey.

One day Lester Patrick, Frederickson's coach and manager, came up with a brilliant solution for dealing with his star player's gift for the gab. He allowed Frederickson 30 minutes a day for nonstop chatter. In Patrick's office each morning Lester would pull out his watch and tell Fredrickson to spout off on any subject. Exactly half an hour later Patrick would call a halt.

It seemed to work as Frederickson poured out his comments and opinions each day across the desk from Patrick, his one-man audience. In time Patrick began to look forward to these daily monologues. That pleased his players. They, in turn, could look forward to half an hour each day without having to listen to a compulsive chatterbox.

The Case of the Missing Towels

FORMER NHL PLAYER Nick Fotiu proudly claims the title "Hockey's Best Practical Joker." In a long career with several different clubs Fotiu tormented hundreds of friends and foes with his impish creations.

129

"I was with Calgary when this happened," he recalls. "Before practice one day I took all the towels stacked up in the dressing room and secretly smeared gobs of Vaseline between the folds. I'd done it before with great success, especially when Lanny McDonald got the Vaseline all mixed in with his huge mustache. It was hilarious. But this time, after the guys had showered and used their towels, there was no reaction. Not one scream of outrage. Something had gone wrong, but I couldn't figure out what.

"I took Bearcat Murray, our trainer, aside and said, 'Bearcat, those towels stacked up outside the showers this morning. I planted a little surprise in them. What the hell happened?'

"He said, 'Geez, Nick, I didn't know that. I took those towels over to the visitors' dressing room. They were for the Vancouver Canucks.'

"I had to laugh when I thought of the Canucks drying off with those towels. I had a vision of them cursing and vowing to get even with the sneaky teammate who'd played such a dirty trick on them."

Another Fotiu gem involves Mark Osborne. "One time, when I was with the Rangers, I caught Mark Osborne about to play a gag on me. We were on a flight and, thinking I was asleep, Mark was about to spray shaving cream on my head. I told him I owed him one and it was going to be a dandy.

"A few days later we were in Vancouver, so I went down to the docks and bought some fish. I cut the fish up into little pieces and stuck the pieces in Mark's uniform, tucking them into little recesses where he wouldn't notice them. The smell wasn't too bad for the first couple of days, but then that uniform really began to reek. Guys wouldn't even sit next to him on the bench. Other players would skate by him holding their sticks like fishing rods, pretending they were casting. Geez, did he stink! That was one of my best efforts."

A Rocky Day
for Perry Turnbull

THE WINNIPEG JETS JOURNEYED to New York a few seasons back, and in this shopping mecca of North America, Jets forward Perry Turnbull spotted a bargain. On a street corner he saw a man selling videotape recorders at what appeared to be a reasonable price. The man was willing to bargain, and Turnbull, pleading limited funds, soon had the price down to $150.

The man hesitated. "Make up your mind," Turnbull said. "I'm with a hockey team and I've got a bus to catch to the airport."

"Sold," the man said, pocketing the cash. "Here's one that's already boxed. It's the same as the model you've been looking at."

Turnbull took his purchase and hurried off to catch the team bus. En route to the airport he told his mates about the bargain price he had paid for a quality VCR.

"Open the box," someone said. "Let's have a look at it."

Turnbull obliged. Inside the box, wrapped in newspapers, was a large stone.

When he reported for practice the next morning, someone had placed two rocks inside his locker. On one the word BETA was printed in bold letters, on the other VHS.

Reporting to Springfield

MY FRIEND RICK BRIGGS-JUDE told me the following stories when we worked together on *Hockey Night in Canada*. Rick is now a successful producer on TSN hockey telecasts.

We were at a Molson hockey luncheon one day when Rick asked, "Brian, did you hear about the two players on the Quebec Nordiques? Seems Pierre Aubrey and J. P. Sauve were demoted to Fredericton of the American Hockey League. And they were told to meet up with the Nords' farm club in Springfield. So they jump on a plane and away they go.

"They jump off the plane when it lands and they grab a cab. 'Take us to the Marriott,' one of them says. The cabbie looks back and says, 'You must be kidding. There's no Marriott in this town.' They look shocked. 'What do you mean?' they ask. 'Isn't this Springfield? Where the hockey team plays?' The cabbie looks at them and says, 'There's no hockey team here that I know about.'

"You know what they did?" Rick asked. "They got on the wrong plane. They went to Springfield, Illinois. They were supposed to be in Springfield, Massachusetts! Can you believe it?"

Rick Briggs-Jude told me another story me about a fight he once witnessed in a game. "Yeah, a brawl broke out in Hartford between the Whalers and the Rangers on Saturday night. Everybody on the ice dropped their gloves and got into it. The fight was winding down and the penalties were being handed out when suddenly one of the Rangers chases after a Whaler and jumps on his back. The Whaler was either Ed Hospodar or Chris Kotsopolous. The Rangers were pissed because he was picking up some of their gloves and stuffing them under his jersey. He was heading off the ice when he was jumped and the gloves fell out. They were Ranger gloves. And he was *stealing* them! The fans thought it was hilarious."

Clinton Rink Needs an Overhaul

SHORTLY AFTER THE TURN OF THE CENTURY the Goderich club laid a complaint against the Clinton, Ontario, rink. A Goderich official stated: "The rink there is not boarded on the sides or the end, eight large beams that cross the rink overhead tend to block the puck when it is lifted down the ice, the space for spectators to stand on is only about a foot wide and people tend to fall out on the ice and interfere with the play at the most inappropriate times."

How did the Clinton rink compare with the rink in St. Thomas, which had also come in for some criticism?

"The rink in St. Thomas is almost as bad. The boards on one side are a few inches off the ice and the puck frequently slides underneath, causing frequent delays."

And the rink in Stouffville?

"Well, it's a disgrace. No team wants to play on a rink that is only 27 feet wide."

Loafers, Gum Chewers Not Wanted

IN 1907 THERE APPEARED to be a couple of players on the Sault Ste. Marie team possessed with what today might be called an "attitude." Their release from the club was reported in the following manner: "Drolet was released last week and Wilson was let go yesterday. The club doesn't pay men to lean against the fence and chew gum while the game is on. Life is too short and the other fellows too quick."

The Trainer Got into the Game

IT WAS THURSDAY, APRIL 20, 1989, at the Calgary Saddledome. The hometown Flames jumped into a 3–0 lead over the visiting Los Angeles Kings in game two of their best-of-seven playoff series.

Then, in a goal-mouth skirmish, Bernie Nicholls of the Kings punched Flames goaltender Mike Vernon in the head, sending him sprawling to the ice. Referee Bill McCreary signaled a delayed penalty as play moved out of the Calgary zone.

That was when Calgary trainer Jim "Bearcat" Murray, reacting to Vernon's injury, leaped over the boards and onto the ice. He dashed straight for Vernon and began administering to him. Meanwhile the Flames were buzzing around the Kings' goal at the other end of the rink. Moments later they were rewarded when Al MacInnis slammed in a goal.

Some of the Kings protested. "Look, their trainer

jumped over the boards while the play was on. Isn't that 'too many men on the ice'?" McCreary, who had never encountered such a situation before, opted for a commonsense decision and allowed the goal to stand.

The NHL's director of officiating, the late John McCauley, said, "I'd never seen anything like it, either. McCreary didn't see Murray come on the ice and he let the play continue. In his judgment he had to count the goal. It was the right call."

Someone who keeps track of such things figured the Flames had an extra man on the ice — Bearcat Murray, the trainer — for about 12 seconds when MacInnis tallied. Murray came in for a lot of postgame kidding from the Flames, but he had the perfect answer. "Boys, all I know is I'm plus one for the playoffs."

Game Delayed — the Coaches Are Missing

DURING THE 1988 Stanley Cup playoffs, in a game between the St. Louis Blues and the Chicago Blackhawks, Chicago coach Bob Murdoch called for a strategy meeting during the first intermission. He and his assistant coaches entered a small room next to the team dressing room. Murdoch was the last man in, so he slammed the door hard behind him. A bit too hard obviously, for when the meeting broke up, none of the coaches could get the door open again. Arena workers arrived on the scene, but they, too, were unable to open the door. Meanwhile the fans were growing restless and many clamored for a resumption of play. Suddenly an unsung hero saved the day. Riding up on a forklift, he wheeled his machine toward the door, crashed into it, and sent it flying. The three coaches stepped over the broken pieces, dusted themselves off, and returned to their coaching duties.

What a Shooter!

PAUL GRANT, 18, of Paducah, Kentucky, was watching a game on television between the U.S. Olympic Team and Czechoslovakia when the Americans scored. Grant, who had been playing with a .38-caliber revolver at the time, became so excited that he pulled the trigger and shot himself in the hand.

"It just went off," he told police. "I tensed up when the puck went in and — bang!"

Language Ban Led to Bernie Parent Trade

FORMER PRO ANDRE LACROIX says a gag order led to Bernie Parent being traded from the Philadelphia Flyers. Lacroix, who led the Flyers in scoring in 1969 and 1970, recalls the events leading up to the deal.

"Vic Stasiuk was coaching the Flyers at that time. He was the worst coach I ever had. One day he called all the French-Canadian players on the team together — there was myself, Jean-Guy Gendron, Simon Nolet, Serge Bernier, and Bernie Parent — and he told us, 'Guys, from now on, no more speaking French. Speak English only.'

136

"We were very upset. Who was Vic Stasiuk to tell us we couldn't speak our language? It wasn't as if we were a clique. We didn't hang around together. We all mixed in with our English teammates.

"What's more, we'd been losing games, and it was almost as if he was blaming the French-speaking players for the losses. So we were disturbed. And we were told not to tell anybody about this edict from Stasiuk.

"But somebody told. And it made all the papers, especially in Quebec where it was front-page news. Stasiuk was called before [NHL president] Clarence Campbell, and he denied he told us we couldn't speak French.

"It was Bernie Parent who leaked the story to the Montreal press. And the Flyers were mad at Bernie

Philadelphia Flyer Bernie Parent being interviewed after Stanley Cup victory in 1974.

(Robert B. Shaver)

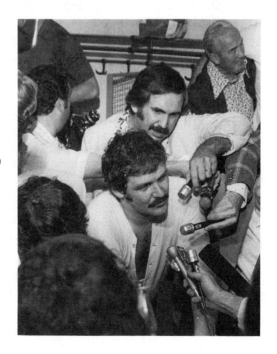

for that. It was one of the biggest reasons they traded him to Toronto in January 1971."

The Flyers didn't stay angry with Bernie very long. They reacquired him in a 1973 trade with the Leafs, and he promptly led Philadelphia to back-to-back Stanley Cups. His jersey number (1) has been retired by the Flyers.

The One-in-a-Million Shot

WHEN DAVE DUNCAN of Oshawa, Ontario, attempted to win $8,000 toward the purchase of a new car in one of those hockey Score-O competitions between periods, he wasn't given a chance. Aside from being legally blind, Duncan was faced with the near-impossible task of shooting a puck three-quarters of the way down the ice surface and through a slot just slightly wider than the puck itself. Duncan, 25, amazed onlookers by sending a perfectly aimed shot through the slot with a one-in-a-million shot.

The Ultimate Free Agent

ANDRE LACROIX, the youngest of 14 children from Lauzon, Quebec, always negotiated his own hockey contracts, both in the NHL and the WHA. And he never made a bad deal. Sitting in the stands at the Hartford Civic Center one day, he told me this fascinating story.

"Let's begin in Philadelphia when I signed with the WHA Blazers in 1973. I negotiated a five-year contract worth $65,000 a year. The previous season

I'd played for Chicago in the WHA — for $30,000 a year. The Blazers had to give me what I wanted because the team had called a press conference for the next day to announce the signing of their new coach — Fred Creighton. But Fred backed out at the last minute. They were really stuck for a news story and they looked to me to become the story. So I asked for a big contract and got it. They really needed me at that press conference. And I made sure there was a clause in the contract that stated if the team was sold or moved I would become a free agent. Also, I demanded a car of my choice — a Mark IV — and I put in a lot of bonus clauses. Well, I won the scoring title that season, made the first All-Star team, and the Blazers had to pay me $40,000 in bonuses.

"Then the team moved to Vancouver, but I didn't have to move there because I was a free agent. I moved to New York instead and negotiated another fat contract with the team there. The next thing I asked for was a new Cadillac, and they said, 'No problem.' So I drove around in my new Cadillac until I got a phone call from the dealer. He said, 'Bring the car in, Mr. Lacroix. The team can't make the payments on it.'

"Within days the New York team moved to New Jersey, and the minute they did I became a free agent again. The New Jersey team was owned by a construction man — Mr. Joe Schwartz. He said to me, 'Andre, we're going to move the team to San Diego.' I said, 'That's fine, but I may not go because I'm a free agent.' So he took me to Las Vegas for three days. I stayed in a big suite while we negotiated a new contract. As usual I was my own agent and I signed a new five-year contract with Joe with all the money guaranteed. And I told Joe I'd like to drive a Porsche as part of the deal. He said, 'No problem.' So I drove a big Porsche until Joe Schwartz ran out of money after a couple of years.

"That's when Ray Kroc [then the owner of McDonald's] came in and bought the club. He hired a big-name baseball man, Buzzy Bavasi, as club president. When Bavasi talked to me about signing, he told me, 'You know, Andre, baseball players, when they make so much money, don't have bonus clauses.' I told him, 'Look, I'm a hockey player, not a baseball player. I want bonus clauses.' I also told him I wanted a Rolls-Royce to drive, one of those $95,000 ones, not a cheap one. Mr. Bavasi said, 'No problem.'

"Kroc and Bavasi offered me $150,000 a year for five years. I said, 'No, I don't want to sign for that. I think I'll go back to the NHL.' And I got up to leave. But Kroc called me back and said, "Andre, I'm prepared to give you $175,000 a year for six years with the money guaranteed personally by me.' I said that sounds okay with me. So I signed a personal services contract with Ray Kroc, not the team or the league.

"It wasn't long before Kroc decided he didn't like hockey, after all, so he sold the team. Once again I became a free agent and I decided to go to Houston. And if Houston at any time didn't pay me, Kroc was still responsible for my contract. When Houston folded and several of the players went to Winnipeg, I didn't go. I was a free agent again, so I went to Hartford. The Whalers promised to honor my contract. If they didn't pay me, Kroc was still responsible.

"When I retired from Hartford, I still had two years left on my contract. I told the Whalers, 'Look, you'll owe me about $400,000 if I continue to play. And I'm not going to retire unless I get my money.

Wheeler dealer Andre Lacroix as a Hartford Whaler, one of many teams he played for in the NHL and WHA.

(Steve Babineau)

So why not do this. You can have the advantage of using that money if you'll pay me over a period of time with interest. And they said fine. So I agreed to be paid over a period of seven years. When I quit in 1980, I knew there would still be plenty of money coming in. What's more, I'd have some time to look around and see what I wanted to do with the rest of my life. And I didn't have to work for the team to earn any of that money. I thought it was a pretty good deal.

"I never had an agent. Never felt I needed one. I made all my own deals and had good relations with all the owners, general managers, and coaches I ever played for — except for Vic Stasiuk in Philadelphia. I never liked him after he ordered the French-speaking players on our team to speak English only."

Dopey Deals

IN JANUARY 1983 the Seattle Breakers of the Western Hockey League traded the rights to forward Tom Martin to Victoria — for a team bus. "It was no big deal at the time," Martin said. "I heard it was a good-looking bus."

On June 18, 1987, New York Ranger GM Phil Esposito announced he had traded a number one draft choice and $100,000 to the Quebec Nordiques for the Nords' coach Michel Bergeron. During Bergeron's second season on the job, Esposito fired him.

How to Dispose of a Dirty Diaper

I ONCE PLAYED a stinker of a gag on a member of my old-timers' team. After a game one day, we showered and dressed, then one of the younger players asked, "Hey, do you mind if I bring my wife and baby into the room? They're out in the corridor waiting for me."

"Bring 'em in," we told him.

So the man's wife came in, and the first thing she wanted to do was change the baby's diaper. She placed the baby on a bench and made the change. But what a load in that diaper! And what a stench in the room! She said, "Oh, dear, what'll I do with this smelly diaper?"

And I said, "No problem. We'll stash it right in this old hockey bag." And that was what I did.

The bag belonged to John Allan Cameron, the well-known Canadian entertainer. But he was in the other room combing his hair or something, and when he came back, his bag was all zipped up and ready to go.

Guess what? He took the bag to the Maritimes with him where he had a gig and where he had been invited to play in a tournament. It was a few days before he opened that bag.

The next time he showed up to play with us he said, "Boys, you got me good. When I opened that bag in Cape Breton to get my equipment, the guys in the dressing room almost bolted for the door. The stench was that bad. And I didn't know why until I spotted that little bundle hidden in among my gear. Thanks to you sons of bitches I'll never get invited to play in Cape Breton again."

Pilous Pulled His Goalie — with Amazing Results

IN THE LATE FIFTIES the St. Catharines Tee Pees were playing the Toronto Marlboros in a critical playoff game. During the last minute of play, with the Marlies leading 5–4, many fans headed for the exits of the St. Catharines Arena. They wanted to beat the rush to the parking lot.

With 28 seconds left on the clock, there was a face-off in the St. Catharines zone. That was when Tee Pees coach Rudy Pilous decided to take his biggest hockey gamble. He pulled his goalie. Netminder Marv Edwards was furious when Pilous waved him to the bench. "Have you lost your friggin' mind?" he squawked. "The face-off is right next to our net."

"Sit down, kid!" Pilous ordered. "Let's see what happens."

Anticipating an easy empty-net goal, the grinning Marlboros couldn't wait for the puck to be dropped. Meanwhile the fans howled their displeasure, and the Tee Pee players glared at the man who appeared to be handing the game to the Toronto boys.

When the puck was dropped, the Marlies pounced on it, all of them eager to fire the disk into the empty net. But somehow it was a Tee Pee who came up with the rubber. Hugh Barlow raced down the ice with 12 seconds to play and banged in the tying goal.

There was bedlam in the arena. In the parking lot fans leaped out of their vehicles and raced back to reclaim their seats for the overtime.

Pilous made all the right moves in overtime. His team won the game and went on to capture the Memorial Cup. Even today in St. Catharines old-timers love to talk about the day Pilous pulled his goaltender and dared the Marlies to score into the nearby empty net.

Who Pulled the Plug?

THE EDMONTON OILERS and the Boston Bruins were locked in a 3–3 tie at the Boston Garden. It was May 24, 1988, the fourth game of the Stanley Cup finals, and 14,500 frantic fans screamed their support for the hometown Bruins. Suddenly the screaming stopped and so did everything else. With 3:23 left to play in the second period, an overload on a 4,000-volt switch knocked out the lights in the run-down old building, leaving players, referees, and fans in the dark. After a long delay, an auxiliary generator was put into use, providing some light, but not enough to play by. Officials evacuated the building, and NHL president John Ziegler declared the game would be replayed in its entirety two nights later in Edmonton. With the unexpected home ice advantage, the Oilers breezed to a 6–3 victory and their fourth Stanley Cup win in the past five years.

Gatecrasher Scores the Winner

FORWARD BILL SUTHERLAND was forced to become a gatecrasher and bull his way into the arena for the home opener of the Philadelphia Flyers the night they made their NHL debut. It was early in October 1968, and Sutherland was eager to suit up for the Flyers' first game in their new home — the Spectrum.

What a surprise when he arrived at the rink! Nobody knew him and nobody would let him in.

"But I'm playing tonight," he protested. "I'm a Flyer."

"Prove it," the man attending the gate snapped.

When Sutherland couldn't produce anything to show he was on the Flyer payroll, he was told to get lost. "Nobody gets in without a ticket," the man at the gate said.

When the attendant turned to look after some paying fans, Sutherland dashed through the gate and ran down the corridor to the Philadelphia dressing room. An hour later, when he skated out to face the Pittsburgh Penguins, he vowed to do something that night to make the fans — and gate attendants — remember him. Early in the third period he scored the only goal of the game to give the Flyers a 1–0 victory.

Barrie Had the Ball Brothers

IT WAS THE FINAL MINUTE of a game in Barrie many years ago, and Bob McLean, the hometown play-by-play announcer, grew extremely excited when the visiting coach pulled his goaltender in an effort to tie the score. But Hap Emms, the Barrie coach, sent two brothers named Ball over the boards to defend against the strategy. McLean told his rapt audience, "Folks, Coach Hap Emms has just put his two Balls out on the ice."

McVie's Misconduct — Skating Too Fast

TOMMY MCVIE, who coached in the NHL and starred as a player in the old Western Hockey League, once drew a misconduct penalty for skating too fast. At least that was what everyone in the building concluded after an incident that took place at the Los Angeles Sports Arena.

The situation was a common one in hockey. The Portland coach, Hal Laycoe, disputed one of referee Lloyd Gilmour's decisions. He ordered McVie to approach the referee and get an interpretation. McVie wasn't called the Clown Prince of the Western League for nothing. He raced at top speed toward Gilmour and threw a foot of snow at Gilmour's feet as he skidded to a stop. Then he bolted back to his team's bench to deliver Gilmour's response. Laycoe had another message for the ref, and McVie flew back over the ice again, throwing more snow when he slammed on the brakes.

By this time the fans were howling with laughter. Even Laycoe started to crack up. But not Gilmour. He brushed the snow from his trousers and gave McVie a 10-minute misconduct.

McVie didn't argue. He turned and raced at full speed toward the penalty box, crashed through the gate, and fell down inside. The confused penalty timekeeper asked him, "What are you in for?"

"Skating too fast, I guess," McVie said, chuckling.

Plante Calls for a Tape Measure

SHORTLY AFTER HE WAS TRADED from the Montreal Canadiens to the New York Rangers in 1963, All-Star goaltender Jacques Plante told his general manager there was something wrong with the goal nets at Madison Square Garden.

"Wrong, Jacques?" was the reply. "What could possibly be wrong?"

"I don't know," Plante admitted. "But I think they may not be the right size. Maybe they're too high or too wide."

"But that's impossible, Jacques. They're all made to standard specifications."

"Let's check them out," Plante said. "I know I'm right."

They took a tape measure out onto the ice and

measured the opening. The standard opening for a goal was four feet by six feet, but the nets in New York were bigger by an inch and a half. The manager was astounded. He discovered that certain manufacturers of goal nets placed the crossbar directly on top of the two upright posts, while others welded it in between the posts, accounting for the inch-and-a-half discrepancy. Plante had been the only goalie to wonder about it, the only one to complain.

"What difference does it make?" a reporter asked. "It all evens out over a season."

"No, it doesn't," Plante argued. "If I play 40 home games in front of a bigger net than the one Glenn Hall protects over 40 games in Chicago, and Hall and I are in the Vezina Trophy race, who do you think has a better chance of winning it? That little extra space may mean as much as 20 goals against in a season. Maybe more."

NHL officials agreed, and immediate steps were taken to measure all the nets used by every team. Several had to be replaced.